Enjoy The Recipes

Regards

JO

And thanks for your help.

Pete Quinlan

HANDS AND HEARTS

Peter Michael Winery

Calistoga, California

2004

Peter Michael Winery
12400 Ida Clayton Road
Calistoga, CA 94515-9507
www.petermichaelwinery.com

ISBN 0-9759212-1-5

Library of Congress Cataloging-in-Publication Data

Hands and hearts / Peter Michael Winery.
p. cm.
"Dedicated to the fight against cancer."--Cover
ISBN 0975921215   ISBN 0975921207 (Collectors ed.)

1. Cookery. 2. Menus. 3. Peter Michael Winery. 4. Wine and wine making – California.
I. Peter Michael Winery. II. Title: Hands and hearts : the passion to create great food and wine.

Printed at Argus Press in Niles, Illinois

First Edition
2004

ACKNOWLEDGMENTS

I am indebted to my father, Mick, who introduced me at a young age to the pleasures of France, especially its food and wine. Without those experiences, the Peter Michael Winery and this book would not have existed.

I am also deeply grateful for the inspiration of my family who share in the excitement of my food and wine passions, both in California and in Europe. A special thank you goes to my wife, Maggie, who has been at my side every step of the way. To the next generation, Paul and Emily (Ma Belle-Fille, our family member editor), and David, I say: May you share friendship and good cheer, and continue the traditions that we have begun.

I would also like to thank the many people, both past and present, who have helped make Peter Michael Winery the success it is today. The quality of the product is a tribute to vineyard manager Javier Aviña and winemakers Luc Morlet, currently our flag carrier, Mark Aubert, and Helen Turley, who all have helped to create and maintain the Peter Michael style. Behind the scenes is a highly committed winery staff including Bill Vyenielo, Joy Henderson, Colleen West, and Herb Westfall.

As an admirer of the graphic arts, I owe thanks to the many photographers who, over the years, have been inspired to document the beauty of the land and the activities of the winery. Among them are Olaf Beckmann, Brian Bloom, Dan Connors, Dan Escobar, Steven Rothfeld, and Penny Wolin.

The personal involvement and support of the chefs and their partners, managers, staffs and sommeliers were instrumental in completing this book. Thank you all with special thanks to Rebecca Cross, Mel Davis, Céline Delany, Georgette Farkas, Patricia Harding, Rachel Hayden, Kristine Keefer, Abigale Knapp, Reinhardt Lynch, Andrew Mckenzie, Mandy Oser, Anna Pedron, Julie Priceman, Carole Saville, Alpana Singh, Patrick Skovran, Mark Slater, Jason Smith, Rochelle Smith, Pattie Strickland, Caroline Styne, and Sari Zernich.

Finally, thanks to you for owning this book.

Sir Peter Michael

Thank you *for choosing this book for your home, thus contributing to cancer research and the support of other selected charities. Cancer has affected my family and united many, so with* Hands and Hearts *we pledge our commitment and support together with you.*

Well over twenty years ago, I was introduced to a mountainous property in Knights Valley. The transformation from cattle ranch to vineyard took two years, the first vines being planted in 1983 and the first vintage released four years later. Little did I know at that time just how much this project would enhance our lives as a family, for Peter Michael Winery has become a wonderful and treasured home and we sincerely hope it will become a legacy for generations to come.

Our wines have received such generous compliments from both consumers and wine connoisseurs, and through this connection we now have the privilege to know the finest chefs and restaurants around the world, where our wines are offered as part of a complete dining experience. This book became a unique opportunity for us to display an insight into the history, the variety, the great art and the dedication of the hands of these chefs and the heart of our winery. It is my hope that you will visit all the restaurants showcased here, perhaps cook the recipes described, and, of course, enjoy it all with our wines!

Hands and Hearts *will give, in more ways than one, to ours and to many other lives in the future.*

Maggie and I thank you for your support.

Sir Peter Michael

HANDS AND HEARTS

Table of contents

Introduction   8

Peter Michael Winery   10

Robert Parker Preface   58

Wine Profiles   60

The Chefs   68

Daniel Boulud   70

John Campbell   78

Tom Colicchio   86

Gary Danko   94

Ken Frank   102

Suzanne Goin   110

Jean Joho   118

Thomas Keller   126

Patrick O'Connell   134

Michel Richard   142

Eric Ripert   150

Guenter Seeger   158

Joachim Splichal   166

Charlie Trotter   174

Norman Van Aken   182

Appendix   190

ON THE BACK LABEL OF EVERY PETER MICHAEL WINE

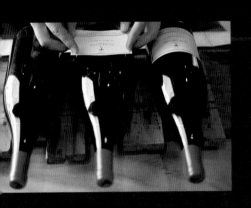

PETER MICHAEL WINERY

In 1982, Peter Michael acquired the square mile

of rocky volcanic ridges in northeast Sonoma County that was to become Peter Michael Winery. The founding of a winery was the fulfillment of a dream. But as so often happens when dreams become real, life's circumstances had made some alterations. In this case, it had moved the dream 6,000 miles to the west.

Peter was born in England in 1938, trained as an engineer and then embarked on a successful career that led to him being knighted by Queen Elizabeth II in 1989 in recognition of his work for government, industry and charity.

Sir Peter and his wife, Lady Michael ("Pete and Maggie"), have two sons, Paul and David. Paul and his wife, Emily, have two children, Elliot and Anna. Any true understanding of Peter Michael Winery begins with the fact that the property is first and foremost a family home.

Pete and Maggie have spent over twenty years on the property building memories, entertaining friends, seeing their children grow up and, in the last few years, enjoying the first visits of grandchildren. It has certainly been a magical place for the children in the family, offering swimming, boating, fishing and endless opportunities to hike and explore the surrounding mountains and forest.

Pete has a vision for the estate he calls "100 by 100," meaning a venture that is 100 percent family-owned for at least 100 years. "If you have spent a lifetime in international business, you need to return to the soil. It's a pretty basic human feeling," says Pete. "Of the many businesses I have founded, this is the only one which carries my family name and I hope it will remain as a legacy for generations to come."

To Pete and Maggie, the key to that legacy is forming an attachment to the land and seeing that the younger members of the family appreciate the wonders of the surroundings. These feelings are echoed in their home in England, where Maggie is the head of a 1,000-acre family estate in Berkshire devoted to farming grain and raising cattle. "It's stewardship of the land," says Maggie. "As the old saying goes, Live as though you are going to die tomorrow, but farm as if you will live forever."

Given the highly personal nature of Pete's commitment, it is not surprising that the profiles of the wines he produces are designed much more to his own taste than to a vision of the marketplace. As it turns out, the marketplace has liked Pete's taste just fine.

With Pete's deeply bred interest in things of quality—sculpture, art, music, food and literature—developing an interest in wine was a short and natural step inspired by the passion of his father. "My father was a great oenophile," says Pete. "He lived in France for many years and we would visit the great vineyards and wine auctions. Our tours took us through some of the very best Burgundian domaines and Bordeaux chateaux." Pete was struck by the regard the French people had for the soil and vines, and the sense of timeless commitment and tradition that permeated these centuries-old estates.

"Of the many businesses I have founded,
this is the only one which carries my
family name and I hope it will remain as
a legacy for generations to come."

When Pete made the decision to look for an estate of his own, it might be expected that his personal experiences would lead him to France, but, again, he was guided by his father's knowledge. "My father wanted a French vineyard in the '60s but found that it could take fifty years to buy fifty good contiguous acres. *Code Napoléon* has worked against keeping vineyards in families."

By then, however, Pete also had another frame of reference: the

wine country of California. His work in high technology businesses had taken him to the San Francisco Bay Area where he spent time in the early boom years of Silicon Valley. He travelled extensively around the region and soon became acquainted with the wine-growing areas in Napa and Sonoma counties to the north. "I looked at the mountains and the rivers and fell for the scene," he says. "That was it, really, although it took a long time, from 1975 to

1982, to actually find anywhere that I liked enough to buy."

Needless to say, he had also discovered California wine. "It happened in a flash one night in San Francisco at the Fairmont Hotel on Nob Hill when I went to see Peggy Lee perform in the Venetian Room," says Pete. Having already sent back two bottles of Bordeaux that were badly corked, he asked the sommelier to recommend a California wine. "He brought a Chateau Montelena Cabernet Sauvignon and it was delicious, and from that point on I was converted. Montelena is the winery that is closest to us here at Peter Michael Winery and was the first from California to win the Paris blind tasting for the 1976 vintage. PMW has had similar successes a few times since."

Pete had some specific requirements for a potential property, "Of course, I was looking for beautiful territory, but it had to be near enough to San Francisco for a drive into the city and back in a day. Then there needed to be water on the property. In California there is plenty of land but without water there is nothing you can do with it. There needed to be a house to work on and sufficient space, too, for a serious project. A square mile seemed a good number and I set my long-time English friend, realtor Angela Rubin, to search for it."

On an April day in 1982, after a trawl through some forty properties, Pete first saw the land that was to become Peter Michael Winery. It was shown to him by Scott Rodde, a Napa businessman who was acting as the agent for the property as a favor to a friend. It was an auspicious meeting for both men. Not only did the property seem to offer everything that Pete was looking for, but it was the beginning of a friendship that continues to this day with Scott serving as president of the winery.

Pete introduced his family to the site on their way to a vacation in Hawaii. "When I saw the ranch it was stunning, sitting under a huge

And so the pieces were in place. The owner was an English businessman with a longing for the land. The models were the ancient chateaux of France. The raw materials—the steep hillsides, the rocky soils, the cool marine breezes—were pure California. Did these constitute a wine-making philosophy? Perhaps not yet, but it was from a synthesis of these three factors that one would grow.

The first improvements that Pete made included a swimming pool,

mountain with the most beautiful and rugged scenery," says Maggie. "A small, rather neglected house sat below, surrounded by nothing but weeds, with 100 head of cattle roaming the 600 acres. I could see it would be a lot of hard work over the coming years if we were to buy this property. At the same time, I could see the beauty that had captured my husband's heart and imagination." Pete signed the contract a short time later.

tennis court and the installation of a fax machine, which in 1983 was new technology. The pool and tennis court reflected a desire for the property to be a place of retreat and relaxation for his family. The fax machine sent the clear message that, while Pete's ownership was destined to be long-distance at times, the ranch would never lack for his attention.

Peter Michael Winery is located in Knights Valley,

a rugged corridor between Sonoma County's Alexander Valley and Napa Valley. Highway 128 forms the western border of the property as it winds toward Calistoga, a few miles away. Along one flank runs Ida Clayton Road, named for the local schoolteacher who taught in the original schoolhouse on the property nearly 100 years ago. Until 1916, it was a toll road, serving as the primary artery through the valley for transporting agricultural goods and the silver ore from the Great Western mine operating on Mount St. Helena.

Flowing through the property is Redwood Creek, one of the healthiest tributaries of the Russian River, with annual runs of native steelhead. The banks of the creek are lined with alders and redwoods and much of the estate is heavily forested. Pete and Maggie have planted over 10,000 redwoods and firs over the years to protect the soil and watershed and to replace the trees lost to foresters in the early 1900s. Towering above all is the 4,300-foot peak of Mount St. Helena, its broad expanse a patchwork of clinging undergrowth and bare rock glowing in hues from white to gold to purple as the sun makes its passage through the sky. It is the tallest peak in Northern California west of the Sierras and Robert Louis Stevenson, who lived in the area in the 1870s, is said to have used its unique profile and vistas as the model for Spyglass Hill in *Treasure Island*.

The lower part of the property forms a narrow corridor running east along Redwood Creek. It contains the main house, a guesthouse, the estate manager's cottage, the winery buildings and offices and the estate's gardens. Further uphill is a large spring-fed reservoir that is used for swimming and boating by the family and friends. Then, as if it were the stem of a bouquet, the corridor blossoms outward into the vineyards growing on the western slopes of Mount St. Helena.

The rest of Kellogg was destroyed by a fire early in the last century, but its spirit lives on in the Michaels' faithful restoration of the ranch house and the period design of the winery buildings. Says Pete, "Our re-creation in the form of a schoolhouse for the office, a barn for red wine production and a hotel for barrel storage is as near to authentic as we could get." Indeed, the office-schoolhouse even has a bell tower and the whitewashed wood buildings look just as likely to have a horse and wagon out front as the winery's pickups.

MALACOMES RANCHO. RES. OF CALVIN H. HOLMES., KNIGHT'S VALLEY, TP, SONOMA CO, CAL.

The junction of Highway 128 and Ida Clayton Road was the site of a 19th-century town called Kellogg. The name still appears on many maps of the area. It was planned as a resort, along the lines of Calistoga, but the inability to get railroad access doomed it to failure. The town and surrounding property were purchased by Calvin Holmes, a wealthy landowner, who named the parcel Sugarloaf Ranch and turned it over to raising cattle. In 1887, he built the Ranch House for his daughter's wedding present. It has survived to become the Michaels' residence.

The Ranch House sits on a hill overlooking the valley floor. Maggie's tireless energy has been the driving force behind the restoration and expansion of the Victorian structure. Her kitchen is designed to evoke a 200-year-old English country house. State-of-the-art appliances are complemented by Queen Anne pine cabinetry, and the rustic space is framed with rough-hewn beams salvaged from a condemned pier on San Francisco Bay. It manages to be at once functional enough for entertaining or supporting large catered events, yet warm and comfortable enough to be a place for the family.

On the south side of the house is a patio with a pool and a hillside garden planted in the Mediterranean style with agapanthus, iris, lavender and canna. Running along the length of the east side is a terrace providing views of Mount St. Helena. Below the terrace are manicured lawns and an informal English garden planted in yew hedges and roses. It is here on the English lawns that performances for charity benefits take place on warm August evenings. Renowned soprano Ruth Ann Swenson was a featured guest at an event held

Acres of plantings fan out from the main house connected by meandering crushed-granite pathways. The gardens, too, have been a focus of Maggie's attention. "Alan Peirson, our first estate manager, was a very enthusiastic and talented gardener," says Maggie. "We had long discussions about how to plan the garden and parkland. Alan knew we wanted a little bit of England there with us and that guided the design, but the unique microclimate determined many of the selections." There is a Japanese garden with rhododendrons,

for the Napa Valley Opera House and the San Francisco Opera. On another magical evening, world-famous cellist Yo-Yo Ma, violinist Pamela Frank and pianist and conductor Jeffrey Kahane played for a gathering in support of the Santa Rosa Symphony. The night was made even more poignant by the presence of the brother and sister of Jacqueline du Pré who were able to hear Yo-Yo Ma perform the Elgar cello concerto on the same Stradivarius their sister used to play.

azaleas, dogwood trees and Japanese maples, but most of the space is given over to flora native to California. Beneath the redwoods and firs are manzanita, *Ceanothus americanus*, cistus and a profusion of California poppies. There are also vegetable and herb gardens to supply the family table, a flower garden to provide cuttings for floral displays and a grove of Manzanilla olive trees that has just provided its first pressing.

Dotted throughout the grounds are numerous sculptures. Pete's passion for the art form and his role as the long-time chairman of the Royal Society of British Sculptors led him to start an artist-in-residence program. The first was John Tinney, who worked in concrete. Tom Scicluna graced a field with giant golden balls, like "brontosaurus eggs." Matsuo Nakajima carved "waves of water" in black granite. Kate Randall worked in steel. Pete encouraged Alan Peirson to pursue his talent for sculpture, and the giant nails in rock, ceramic and bronze seen throughout the grounds have become Peirson's trademark, leading him to a career as an artist. "I have liked sculpture for a long time," says Pete. "It seems to have a feel and look that speaks to the engineer in me. You can touch it, walk around it and even sit on some of it."

Be they artists-in-residence, interns working and studying at the winery or visiting relatives and friends, Pete and Maggie gain a great deal of satisfaction from sharing the pleasures of life on the ranch. "There are many people from Europe and the United States whose only perception of California has been gleaned from television shows," says Pete. "Over the years, I'd say upwards of 1,000 people have come to stay at the ranch and gained a new, first-hand impression of how wonderful this part of the country is."

Pete and Maggie's son David reflects on life at the ranch: "I remember going for hikes up the creek with Alan to see what creatures we could find; Jet-Skiing on the lake and early morning misty swims; the day we climbed Mount St. Helena, going up the fire breaks on our hands and knees and sliding back down on our bums; the black widow spider I kept in a jar having babies in my bedroom; the stars on a clear night, getting

out the telescope to see the rings of Saturn, the moons of Jupiter and the Orion nebula."

For all the cultivated grounds and the careful tending by Estate Manager Herb Westfall, there are constant reminders that the estate is part of a wild and living mountain. Black-tailed deer abound, requiring fencing of the vineyards. There are bobcats, coyotes, raccoon

possums and skunks. Red-tailed hawks and turkey buzzards ride the thermals above, wild turkeys roost in the trees and great blue herons and snowy egrets preside over the creek and reservoir, which is plentifully stocked with smallmouth bass, catfish and turtles. Taking an early morning run may very well lead to an encounter with a mountain lion. "There was a pride of three in the vineyards this year," says Vineyard Manager Javier Aviña. At dusk, western diamondback rattlesnakes stretch out on the gravel roads to soak up the last of the afternoon's warmth. And there is a particularly notorious black bear whose appetite for grapes has foiled any attempts to block his access to the vineyards, and whose nose for the ripeness of the fruit often tallies more closely with the taste of the winemakers than do the readings of the Brix scale.

The first vineyard, at 1,100 feet, is called L'Après-Midi (The Afternoon). Pete had it planted to Sauvignon Blanc in 1995, though there was some skepticism on the part of the team whether or not the American public would ever embrace the light, aromatic varietal. "I knew the Loire valley in France and parts of Bordeaux produce superb white wines," says Pete. "It took a while for the winery to discover that California can produce the same level of quality and flavor." The name was suggested by Scott Rodde's daughter, Heather, who had been studying French, and it refers to the fact that the wine is ideal to drink any time after noon. As Pete often points out, "it is always afternoon somewhere."

Next comes Les Pavots Vineyard (The Poppies), named after the California state flower that grows in the area and serves as the logo for Peter Michael Winery as well as the Michaels' Vineyard at Stockcross hotel and restaurant in England. Planted in 1983, the Cabernet Sauvignon, Cabernet Franc, Merlot and Petit Verdot vines grow from 1,100 to 1,500 feet and provide the grapes for the winery's celebrated Red Bordeaux Cuvée.

Further up the mountain, the higher and cooler elevations provide a perfect environment for Chardonnay. La Carrière (The Quarry) is named for its rocky soils that force the vines to struggle to survive and impart a distinctive mineral quality to the grapes. It was planted in 1995 on a southern exposure and rises to 1,800 feet. With some vines on slopes of up to forty-five degrees, it is the most challenging vineyard on the estate to farm.

The oldest Chardonnay vineyard is Belle Côte (Beautiful Slope), named by Pete after the famous ski run in Courchevel, France. It was planted in 1990 on a gently sloping shelf between 1,700 and 1,800 feet. In addition to its cooling elevation, hot temperatures late in the growing season are mitigated by the vineyard's eastern exposure, thereby keeping the fruit out of the potent afternoon sun. The clay and river rock in its soil further differentiates its terroir from La Carrière.

The youngest and highest vineyard on the estate is Ma Belle-Fille (My Daughter-in-Law), named in honor of Emily. It was cleared in 1997, the year of her marriage to Paul, and rises to an elevation of almost 2,000 feet. "Some girls have music composed for them or a flower named in their honor," says Pete. "Emily has a vineyard and  a wine that I think will become among the very best PMW will ever produce." On the back label of the first vintage of Ma Belle-Fille, there is a simple message from Pete and Maggie to Emily: "It is named after a beautiful young woman who is - 'Ma Belle-Fille' - having a delightful perfume and an aromatic flavor that will mature into something very special in just a few years just like its namesake."

The views from the highest vineyards are breathtaking, stretching across Knights Valley toward Napa to the south and extending the breadth of Sonoma County to the west. Down below, the vineyards undulate over the terrain and wrap like a ribbon around the base of Sugarloaf, the hill that gives the property its name. Peregrine falcons nest in the rocky crags above and glide almost motionless on the breeze. It's a good place to be at cocktail time, enjoying a glass of Peter Michael wine. On the rare days when winds from the east push back the marine haze, it's possible to catch a glimpse of the Pacific Ocean over thirty miles away. Climb a little higher with a good pair of binoculars, and you might just make out the clock tower of the Ferry Building on San Francisco Bay.

In a letter to his grandson, Elliot, Peter describes the estate this way. "It is quite the most fantastic place on earth and I am pretty certain

there is nothing else that combines the unique mixture of things that can be found here." It is the mixture of careful cultivation with wilderness. It is the mixture of art and nature. It is the mixture of respect for the past with an appreciation for innovation and technology. And finally, it is the mixture of what wine aficionados know as Peter Michael Winery with the home of a family that always has and always will refer to it simply as Sugarloaf Ranch.

As Pete took the first steps toward founding Peter Michael Winery,

he admits he was "a wine lover who didn't know a great deal about the process of making wine." But he did know what he liked. Pete is a firm believer in the concept of Noble Grapes, the *Vitis vinifera*. These important grape varieties are acknowledged to produce the world's greatest wines. The group includes Sauvignon Blanc, Chardonnay, Riesling, Merlot, Pinot Noir and Cabernet Sauvignon. Of those, Burgundy- and Bordeaux-style wines had been his favorites dating back to his travels in France. "Others may come and go," says Pete. "But the Noble varieties will go on forever." The choice of the Sugarloaf Ranch property was inspired. The climate and soil are ideal for producing the grapes of Burgundy and Bordeaux. The estate's mountainous terrain is also pivotal to the quality of Peter Michael wines, yet, at the time of his purchase, the fact that mountain vineyards produce more intensely flavored fruit was far from common knowledge in California. "In France, I had noticed that the cows were always on the valley floor and the

vineyards were on the hillsides," says Pete. "I didn't know the technical reasons why, but the image stuck with me."

While Pete's understanding of the winemaking process may have been limited, his business acumen was not, and it led him to set forth clear goals for the winery. He was committed to a wine growing philosophy modeled on the French tradition, with barrels and methodology to come from France. "What I hoped to be able to do in the '80s was to show that the then-general preference to choose French wines was misplaced," says Pete. "I am very pleased to find that in the '90s and this millennium, California has become known as the place where great wines can be consistently produced, some of them from Peter Michael Winery." At the time, this was no small gamble, for it relied on the belief that American tastes would grow and evolve to appreciate wines with a more subtle and elegant profile.

He was also determined to never compromise quality out of a desire for growth or widespread market acceptance. "There are people who are very good at working in the mass market," says Pete. "I've never done that in any of my businesses. They've always been aimed for the use of about 1 percent of the population."

Lastly, Pete understood marketing and the crucial importance of choosing the right name for the winery to be. He felt that a single brand name was needed. After much family discussion, he agreed to use his own name and the 'Peter Michael' brand was established. Everything that came from his winery would carry his name up front, regardless of variety or color, and he intended to make that name synonymous with the highest quality.

The respected designer, Chuck House, was brought in to create the packaging. After much exploration, a bottle and label design emerged that was simple yet elegant, projecting confidence without gloss. "I think we made good decisions," says Pete. "We've never needed or wanted to change it."

In 1983, the first vineyard at Sugarloaf Ranch was planted to Cabernet Sauvignon, Merlot and Cabernet Franc. It would be nearly a decade before the fruit of this labor would yield dividends in the production of a world-class 'claret.' One problem was the rootstock, AXR-1, which at the time was believed to be resistant to phylloxera. The resistance proved to be temporary, and a costly replanting of those first twenty acres was required later. The second

was simply the realities of growing red wine. "Red wine needs to be aged longer and the vines really have to be older to impart the flavors—the familiar *vieilles vignes* (old vines) on the labels of French chateau bottles tell the story," says Pete. "The white wine production cycle is shorter and the wines can be enjoyed sooner. Chardonnay, in particular, is capable of producing the best of wines early on."

By 1987, Pete was ready for his first vintage and he hired Helen Turley as winemaker in time for the harvest. His marching orders to Helen were simple but challenging. "I've got a cellar full of the best of Burgundy and Bordeaux," Pete said. "I'm only interested in making wines that could be put on the table next to those. Can you do that?" Helen said yes. She had a purist approach to winemaking, believing in producing wine in limited quantities from single vineyard sites, while allowing the vineyard to express its *terroir* with a minimal amount of intervention from the winemaker. She was also interested in the potential of natural fermentation, where fermentation is carried out by the yeast naturally occurring on the grapes rather than with the addition of industrial yeast. She located some grapes that met her approval on the Gauer Ranch high above Alexander Valley. The first Chardonnay from Peter Michael Winery was ready in time for Peter's fiftieth birthday party. Pete decided to call it Mon Plaisir (My Pleasure), establishing the theme of simple French names that has been extended to all of the winery's offerings. "I am European after all," says Pete. "And I like the idea of paying homage at the same time as providing a little competition."

Chardonnay juice fresh from the grape press at harvest.

FRANÇOIS FRERES

TONNELLERIE

ST ROMAIN   CÔTE D'OR

FRANCE

P M

A

H T

98-042

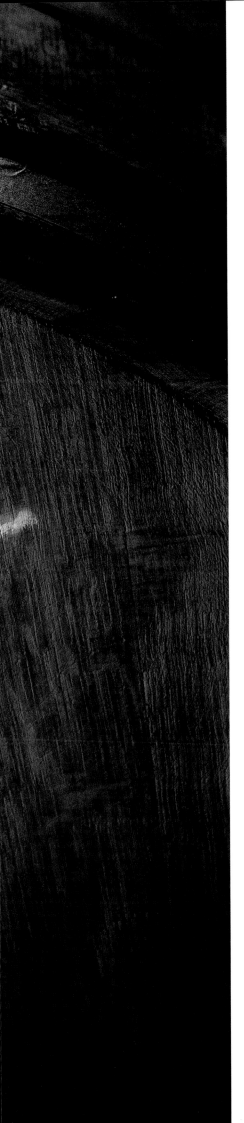

The winery's first Chardonnays met with instant critical acclaim. The fruit was elegantly balanced, rather than overpowering, and the distinctive qualities of each vineyard came forward to provide a uniquely identifying profile. "I've done my utmost over the years to protect and maintain that style," says Pete.

Early on, a practice was developed of setting aside a few select barrels of Mon Plaisir for extra aging on the lees. For identification, the barrels were marked with a red Avery dot sticker. This was the origin of Point Rouge, which has evolved to become a select blend of the finest Chardonnay from the Peter Michael vineyards and is one of the winery's most celebrated cuvées. "We had a bit of a struggle with the BATF, who control wine labeling and initially refused to allow white wine to be labeled 'rouge,'" says Pete. "The same thing happened when we introduced Point Blanc, the red wine that is made only in occasional years. But when we pointed out that Cheval Blanc is one of the world's top red wines from France, they backed down."

Since its inception, there have been three notable winemakers at Peter Michael Winery. The first was Helen Turley who, although she was with the winery for only a short time, established the initial style of the Chardonnays.

Mark Aubert joined the winery as assistant winemaker during Helen's tenure and was chosen as her successor. He stayed for a decade, introduced the first vintages of the red Bordeaux blend, Les Pavots, and improved the quality year after year. Mark retains a consultative winemaking brief with Peter Michael Winery and has gone on to produce his own superb range of wines. After a long search, Luc Morlet was selected for the position of winemaker in 2001.

Luc grew up as part of a winemaking family in Avenay-Val d'Or in the Champagne region of France. Along with master's degrees in winemaking and wine business from Rheims University and Dijon Business School, Luc has worked at vineyards and wineries in Burgundy, Bordeaux, the southwest of France and the Napa Valley. As much as his formal training, Luc's childhood working and playing in his family's vineyard makes him ideally suited for the Peter Michael style. He describes himself as a "terroiriste." Quite simply, he's used to getting to know the vines as if they were his backyard.

Over several years, Mark and Vineyard Manager Javier Aviña oversaw the planting or replanting of all of the estate's Chardonnay, Sauvignon Blanc and red Bordeaux vineyards. In turn, this established Peter Michael Winery as a producer of predominantly estate-grown wines. Needless to say, this was a period of significant investment. Pete figures his mountain vineyards cost twice as much to farm while providing less than half the yield of a valley vineyard, to say nothing of the cost of preparing and planting the vineyards themselves. Yet as the vines struggle to survive in the thin, rocky soil, they produce small berries of unmatched flavor and intensity.

As the style of the wines was being established, Pete and Maggie embarked on the planning and construction of the estate's winery buildings. They decided to emulate the architecture of the old town of Kellogg. Using vintage photographs for inspiration, Chuck House created the designs for the office and wine production buildings.

Bill Vyenielo was hired in 1991 to serve as general manager of the rapidly growing enterprise. He brought a unique depth of experience on both the business and production sides of winemaking, and his ability to reconcile the two has proven critical to a winery that is driven more by philosophy than the marketplace. In typically understated style, Bill says, "The key was just getting out there and letting people taste the wine. Once that happened, the market took care of itself." Pete has a slightly different view. "Bill is a superb manager, and his contributions have had an enormous impact on the business."

Meanwhile, Mark continued and expanded the experiments with natural fermentation, culminating in the release of Cuvée Indigène. Belle Côte was introduced as the winery's first estate-grown Chardonnay. The Chardonnay called La Carrière made its debut in the 1997 vintage. The first Sauvignon Blanc, named L'Après-Midi, came from a vineyard high on Howell Mountain and then the grape source was shifted to the Peter Michael estate in 1997

when the L'Après-Midi vineyard on Mount St. Helena matured.

In January of 1997, a comprehensive blind tasting of virtually every 1994 Montrachet was held at the Hôtel de Crillon in Paris. Robert Parker, Jr., and his assistant were the only two Americans invited to join the French domaines owners, their winemakers and two key Belgian tradesmen on the thirty-three-member panel. Unknown to anyone, Mr. Parker inserted the 1994 Peter Michael Point Rouge Chardonnay. When the results came in, the group had unanimously rated Point Rouge the top wine. "One can well imagine how much this pleased the French," says Pete smiling.

It was during this period that the red Bordeaux blend, Les Pavots, came into its own. A string of vintages from 1992 through 1997 earned the kind of accolades that had always been enjoyed by Peter Michael white wines, and Mr. Parker called the 1996 and 1997 Les Pavots "the two finest efforts I have ever tasted." Pete finds the development of the red wines particularly satisfying. "It's no use starting in this business when you reach retirement. It can take a lifetime to create a top growth Cabernet Sauvignon. Fortunately, I was just young enough. Now, as for my grandchildren, they're the perfect age to start."

The introduction of Le Moulin Rouge, a rich Pinot Noir 'Burgundy' came with the 1997 vintage and has improved with each vintage since. Pinot Noir has a delicacy that often defeats the winemaker and there are only a few California vineyards that produce top-quality vintages. Now, Peter Michael Winery is one of them. Le Moulin Rouge is a Paris cabaret which, since 1889, has been offering sensual delights mixed with excess, as immortalized in the paintings of Toulouse-Lautrec. "I couldn't think of a better name for this wine," says Pete.

With Le Moulin Rouge, Peter Michael Winery extended its offering to include all of the classic varietals of Burgundy and Bordeaux. The initial release from the youngest and highest estate Chardonnay vineyard, Ma Belle-Fille and a fifty-acre parcel in Seaview on the cool Sonoma coast are planned for the future. Says Pete, "We now have a wide range of wines and almost all of them come from our property and our farming procedures. This project and all its continuous extensions have been the most satisfying for more years than I can remember." What had begun twenty years ago as a dream has become a reality—the wines are recognized and sought after by wine lovers the world over and the Peter Michael brand, the only one of the dozens of companies that Pete has founded that bears his name, has more than lived up to the standards of quality that he asked of it.

Peter Michael Winery follows a "neoclassical" winemaking approach,

combining new world innovation with the time-honored traditions of the best French *grand cru* producers. It is an approach based on minimal intervention. The winery's gentle handling of the grapes, fermenting with indigenous yeast and not fining or filtering the wines are all efforts to achieve the most natural and authentic vineyard expression possible. There is irony in the term "minimal intervention," for to carry it out requires careful planning, innovation, an enormous amount of labor on the part of the vineyard crew and passionate attention from the winemaking team.

The process begins in the planning of the estate's vineyards themselves. Each has been carefully sited based on soil conditions, drainage, microclimate and sun exposure. In spite of slopes of up to forty-five degrees, no terracing has been used. Ground cover is planted between the vineyard rows to prevent erosion, attract beneficial insects and draw more harmful insects away from the vines. In turn, clonal selections are made based on each vineyard's unique conditions and the vision for the finished wine. For example, Belle Côte is planted in equal portions to See, Old Wente and Rued clones, whereas its neighboring vineyard, La Carrière, is predominantly the best Dijon clones, with the balance in Hyde and See.

A drive up to the vineyards gives one a quick appreciation of how difficult they must be to farm. The winery's four-wheel drive vehicle climbs two miles of road carved precariously from the hillsides. There are few places to turn around and even fewer where the maneuver seems sensible. In the vineyards, there are slopes where it is simply impossible to stand without planting a firm downhill leg and leaning in to the hillside. A simple tumble in La Carrière could well end up 500 feet below in L'Après-Midi. Yet the work does indeed go on, with crewmembers climbing the hillsides, sometimes on hands and knees, gently tending or guiding the vines by hand.

Luc and Javier oversee a skilled and dedicated crew in the year-round process of maintaining healthy and balanced vines. From the pruning that prepares the vines for winter dormancy to harvest, there are a total of fourteen direct on-the-vine tasks. Tying, two suckerings, two shoot positionings, removal of laterals, leafing, three hedgings and three thinnings are all performed on the steep slopes by hand and in a constant race with time as the vines move from one stage of development to another. The results are healthy root systems and canopies, a small crop of slowly ripening, intensely flavored fruit and a clean, aerated fruit zone.

steep vineyards and a smooth, gentle ride down the mountain. When the lugs are emptied onto the belt of the cluster-sorting table at the crush pad, it is rare to see even a single drop of juice. The pitch of the cluster-sorting table has been calibrated to aid in the placement of the clusters on the belt, thus avoiding damage, and to deliver the fruit directly to the press for white wines or to the destemmer for red wines.

When Luc and Javier (and the bear) agree that full ripeness is reached, the harvest begins. The optimum moment for picking varies from vineyard to vineyard, block to block, even vine to vine, but it typically begins with the white wine grapes in early September and runs six to eight weeks to finish with the Bordeaux reds. Hot weather, which is common at that time of year, accelerates maturation and often requires harvesting at night. Harvest is an arduous, nonstop sprint to keep pace with the progress of nature, and its conclusion is celebrated with a dinner on the crush pad for the entire Peter Michael Winery staff.

As the grape clusters are gently handpicked, a series of innovations are put into play to ensure that the fruit preserves its integrity and quality. The clusters are placed in twenty-eight-pound capacity plastic 'lugs' that can be stacked without any compaction of the fruit, and are constantly protected from the sun by an overhead cover. The lugs are loaded on trailers made exclusively for the winery with special suspension systems that allow for towing through the

When the red wine grapes exit the destemmer, they are spread on the belt of the berry-sorting table. In this innovation by Mark Aubert, the grapes pass by twenty discerning hands and eyes. Bits of stem, which impart bitterness to the wines, and damaged fruit are discarded and only the perfect berries move on to the fermenters. Here the gentle handling continues with a smooth pumping-over regime that increases skin contact during fermentation and aerates the wine.

Unlike industrial yeast, which works in ten to fourteen days, natural fermentation is a temperamental process that can take weeks, or even months, and requires constant vigilance on the part of Luc and his team. After the wine leaves the fermenters, the pomace is removed by hand and gently squeezed in a vertical press with the press wine flowing by simple gravity into barrels. Luc can then use this fractioned press wine as an additional flavor element as he composes the Les Pavots blend of Cabernet Sauvignon, Merlot, Cabernet Franc, and Petit Verdot. The blend is then placed in carefully

selected and toasted French oak barrels where it will age for sixteen to twenty-four months. After bottling, it will age another eight to ten months before its release. During the aging process, the racking of all red wines is carried out by gravity, from one barrel to another, through the 'esquive' side hole. Once again, it is the most gentle of possible techniques to ensure the wine retains its natural integrity.

Through selective picking, each of the estate's Chardonnay vineyards is divided into about twenty lots. These lots receive gentle pressings to extract the juice that goes directly into oak barrels to undergo natural fermentation. Says Luc, "Within these six to eight barrel lots, each barrel of wine has its own characteristics. This diversity provides a great palette of flavors, aromas, texture and concentration with which we compose each wine."

With the exception of the Sauvignon Blanc, all of the Peter Michael wines also undergo a secondary, or malolactic, fermentation. This helps to stabilize the wine, brings softness and complexity and further reduces the need for filtration. As the white wines age, they are given a weekly *bâtonnage,* a stirring of the lees. Putting the lees back in suspension adds what Luc calls *gras* (fat), or flesh, to the mid-palate of the wine and increases its aromatic complexity. The head of one of the winery's barrels has been replaced with glass so the team can observe first-hand the results of the bâtonnage and time the next stirring accordingly.

Luc and his team constantly taste the wines as they move through each stage of their lives. "At Peter Michael Winery there is no pre-written recipe for making the wines," says Luc. "Each year, we base decisions on the characteristics of that vintage. If we're able to eliminate a winemaking manipulation, we don't hesitate to do so. One of my favorite wine anthems is, 'The art of winemaking only starts when one has overcome the techniques.'"

It is impossible to understand the combination of experience, familiarity, taste and inspiration that the team brings to judging and blending the wines, but the highly sensual nature of the task is clear even to a layman visiting the winery. As one climbs through the vineyards, there is the heat of the sun beating down, the crunch of the gravely soil, the smell of the warm earth rising up to mix with the vital green odors of the vines and the refreshing coolness of the ocean breeze. This is the *terroir*. A walk through the mist in the barrel storage rooms tells a different sensual story, cool and full of the aromas of fruit. There is the smell of seasoned oak, the floral, green apple tang of aging whites and the deep, penetrating fruit fragrance of aging Les Pavots. Peter Michael wines have become famous by striking an elegant balance between the two—the unique voice of the vineyard and the flavor intensity of the California grape.

When the time comes to craft finished wines, the team judges each barrel based on its ability to capture the essence of the vineyard and what they have found to be the particularity of that year's vintage. There are no set goals for quantity; the size of each wine's production is based purely on quality and the team's vision for the blend. In turn, only the most exceptional barrels of Chardonnay will be marked with the red sticker that earns them additional aging on the lees and a possible contribution to Point Rouge. In 2001, sixteen barrels were marked and twelve were used. In other years, there have been as few as six. In 2000, the decision was made not to bottle any Point Rouge at all.

At Peter Michael Winery, the past, present and future are as elegantly fused as the flavors of one of its blended wines. The vineyards are farmed by hand. The wines are crafted using centuries-old French techniques. The buildings are an homage to nineteenth-century California. Yet the process is eased through numerous innovations with the use of today's technology.

As for the future, that is where Pete and Maggie have always fixed their gaze. Once it was envisioning the winery that has come to pass. Next it was anticipating the day when their wines would compete with the best of Burgundy and Bordeaux on a world stage. Today, they are working to develop reliable channels so that theirs and other outstanding California wines can be enjoyed in the UK and Europe. And tomorrow? That is for Pete and Maggie's most personal vision of all: to see new generations of the Michael family making wine in Knights Valley.

Robert M. Parker, Jr.'s

The Wine Advocate, Inc.

Main Office
Robert M. Parker, Jr.
P.O. Box 311
Monkton,
Maryland 21111
Tel (410) 329-6477
Fax (410) 357-4504

It is an honor to write this brief preface. Obviously, I love wine and food, but to participate in this project is immensely gratifying, and I am thrilled to have been asked. As readers will easily discern, this book is a cooperative effort with an undeniably noble purpose ... to help save lives.

From the outset, the *purpose* of the book was to raise money for cancer research and other select medical and social causes. I wholeheartedly support this effort. For personal reasons, I have helped raise over two million dollars for the Children's Hospital of Seattle. I believe that it is important for all of us to "give back" in some way, especially those in a position to do so.

I also like the *premise* of the book, and it's one that I can relate to from personal experience. *Hands and Hearts* is more than a celebration of great food and wine. It celebrates the pursuit of passion and using that passion to bring benefit to other peoples' lives. In my case, I began my career as an attorney for the US Government. But I pursued my passion for wine, and for the last twenty-five years it has become the focus of my life and livelihood. It doesn't matter what your calling is - a surgeon, a sculptor, an architect, a chef - when you are moved by what you do, you hope you can move others, and at the same time, give something back to your community, and by extension, your country.

Obviously, I have tasted all of Peter Michael Winery's vintages since the first in 1987. I am also familiar with the fine, creative talents of the chefs featured in this book, many of whom are the culinary prodigies of our era. It was a great pleasure to write the tasting notes that aided the chefs' creativity in the dishes showcased here.

Signed,

Robert M. Parker, Jr.
Author and publisher of *The Wine Advocate*

Additional Office

Washington D.C.
1800 Hoban Rd., NW
Washington, DC 20007
202.333.7165 Tel
202.333.7091 Fax

Since 1978, The Consumer's Independent Guide to Fine Wine

"You can have all the vision, philosophy, skill and experience you want but, in the end, all that really matters is what's in the bottle."

— *Sir Peter Michael*

2001 La Carrière Chardonnay
Estate Vineyard, Knights Valley, Sonoma County

La Carrière is French for "the quarry," a name given to the vineyard for its bowl shape and tremendously rocky soils. It is also the steepest vineyard on the estate, with slopes of up to forty-five degrees. These features are responsible for the exceptional high-toned mineral aspects that characterize the wine.

Robert Parker, Jr.: "The knock-out 2001 Chardonnay La Carrière offers honeyed citrus, liquid mineral, floral, and exotic tropical fruit characteristics as well as admirable definition, texture, body, and richness. Although I suspect the acids are high, the wine is more concentrated than the 2000 with more depth as well as fruit. This brilliant effort should age nicely for 5-8 years."

Belle Côte (Beautiful Slope) was the first estate-grown Chardonnay offered by Peter Michael Winery, and, from the beginning, displayed the unique potential of the property's mountain vineyards. The clay and river rock in its soil differentiates its terroir from La Carrière.

Robert Parker, Jr.: "The 2001 Chardonnay Belle Côte exhibits exotic tropical fruit notes, a layered, opulent texture, medium to full body, less minerality than La Carrière, beautiful layers of fruit, and a stunning finish. This brilliant effort should drink well for 5-7 years."

2001 Cuvée Indigène Chardonnay
Sonoma County

Cuvée Indigène means "naturally fermented cuvée." The origins of the wine go back to the late 1980s when Peter Michael Winery first began experimenting with the use of natural fermentation. Begun as a ten-barrel experiment in 1990, Cuvée Indigène has become a mainstay of the Peter Michael offering and the use of indigenous yeast fermentation has expanded to all of the winery's Chardonnay cuvées.

Robert Parker, Jr.: "The blockbuster 2001 Chardonnay Cuvée Indigène possesses an oily, unctuous texture in addition to smoky, leesy, peach, honeysuckle, and lemon zest aromatics, and dense, deep, full-bodied flavors with great texture, richness, and purity. It is a superb Chardonnay to enjoy over the next decade."

2001 Le Moulin Rouge Pinot Noir
Santa Lucia Highlands, Monterey County

The source for Le Moulin Rouge is the Pisoni Vineyard on the slopes of the Santa Lucia Highlands in Monterey County. Named for the Paris cabaret, the wine's dense, yet delicate richness awakens the senses.

Robert Parker, Jr.: "The 2001 Pinot Noir Le Moulin Rouge (421 cases) could pass for a 1999 Domaine de la Romanée-Conti Richebourg or a 1990 La Tâche...it's that spectacular. It boasts a saturated dark ruby/purple tinged color as well as great intensity (100% destemmed fruit is utilized) and a knock-out nose of forest floor, plums, figs, macerated black cherries, and lilacs. As this magnificent Pinot Noir sits in the glass, even more complex notes of wild cherries and raspberries as well as a touch of kirsch emerge. It is a stunning effort to drink over the next 5-7 years."

2001 L'Après-Midi Sauvignon Blanc
Estate Vineyard, Knights Valley, Sonoma County

Initially produced from a vineyard on Howell Mountain, L'Après-Midi is now grown solely from a small vineyard on the Peter Michael estate. L'Après-Midi means "afternoon," a name given to the wine because its bright, aromatic character can be enjoyed any time during or after lunch.

Robert Parker, Jr.: "Honeyed grapefruit, citrus, and a whiff of melon characterize this medium-bodied, crisp, zesty Sauvignon Blanc. Enjoy it over the next 1-2 years."

2001 Les Pavots Red Bordeaux Cuvée
Estate Vineyard, Knights Valley, Sonoma County

The 2001 Les Pavots is unique from all previous vintages of Les Pavots, as it heralds the first introduction of Petit Verdot to the previously traditional blend of Cabernet Sauvignon, Merlot, and Cabernet Franc.

Robert Parker, Jr.: "The stunning 2001 Les Pavots is a full-bodied, intense example revealing a saturated purple color, and sweet blackberry, cassis, smoke, and licorice aromas. This seamless, plump, and long offering will be at its apogee between 2005-2020. Production was low, with only 2,003 cases produced."

1997 Les Pavots Red Bordeaux Cuvée
Estate Vineyard, Knights Valley, Sonoma County

Les Pavots (The Poppies) is the winery's Bordeaux blend of Cabernet Sauvignon, Merlot, and Cabernet Franc from the estate vineyard on the slopes of Mount St. Helena. The rocky, rhyolitic soils contribute a mineral richness and add to the wine's complexity.

Robert Parker, Jr.: "A blue/black/purple color is followed by an extraordinary bouquet of toast, blackberries, crème de cassis, licorice, and cedar. Full-bodied, with silky tannin, low acidity, and layers of concentrated, pure black fruits judiciously wrapped in subtle toasty oak, this wine can be drunk early, but promises to hit its peak in 5-7 years, and last for two or more decades."

THE CHEFS

DANIEL BOULUD

When asked what his last meal would be, Daniel Boulud says he would choose the homegrown chicken and vegetables and his father's home-cured ham from the farm outside Lyon where he grew up. While this may sound like simple fare for the renowned chef and owner of Daniel, one of the world's finest restaurants, it is entirely consistent with Boulud's character

and culinary philosophy. His heart and his tastes are firmly grounded in the French countryside of his boyhood. He's famous for taking peasant ingredients like sardines, anchovies, and pork bellies and transforming them into princely repasts. And his devotion to the freshest local ingredients available at each time of the year has led him to create full menus of signature dishes for each of the four seasons. In short, Chef Boulud's choice of a final menu is really not simple at all—not as long as he's doing the cooking.

After several years as the celebrated executive chef at Le Cirque, Boulud opened the original Daniel on Manhattan's Upper East Side in 1993. At the beginning of 1999, Daniel moved to its sumptuous new quarters in the former Mayfair Hotel on Park Avenue and 65th Street. The restaurant is designed to be reminiscent of a Venetian Renaissance palazzo, and the 120-seat main dining room, the bar and lounge area, and banquet room feature high coffered and stenciled ceilings with mahogany beams, carved pilasters and balustrades, and custom furnishings with richly textured fabrics. The atmosphere is the height of elegance, yet the soft lighting and warm colors exude comfort. "My dream is to give my guests a dining experience that awakens all the senses," says Boulud.

The menu is rich in choices, with a dozen appetizers and main courses, daily market offerings, four- and five-course tasting menus, and an eight-course grand degustation menu. Signature specialties include creamy oyster velouté with lemongrass and caviar, and roasted squab stuffed with foie gras and morels. Yet the menu constantly evolves with the seasons. In autumn, earthy white truffles from northern Italy appear in dishes such as risotto with porcini. Winter brings the black truffles from Périgord in recipes such as Maine sea scallops layered with black truffle in golden puff pastry. Spring is highlighted by dishes featuring asparagus, morels, and delicate peas, and summer becomes a celebration of fragrant tomatoes, chanterelles, and local sweet corn. The dessert menu is really two, with one section devoted entirely to chocolate creations such as chocolate bombe with a passion fruit crème brûlée center.

Boulud's cuisine is ceaselessly inventive, drawing on influences from all over the Mediterranean, India, and Japan, yet always rooted in French tradition. Each innovation is kept in perfect balance as he enriches rustic dishes with luxurious refinements or adds a contemporary touch to a classic recipe. That same balance is evident in the service, which is so confident and expert that it manages to create a feeling of relaxation and comfort without sacrificing tradition or formality. The wine list offers more than 1,600 selections drawing from a cellar with a 25,000-bottle capacity. The cornerstone is red Bordeaux, with impressive verticals in both first-growths and second-growths, but the list spans 15 countries and also features some of California's rarest and finest wines.

Chef Boulud's energy and industry have resulted in two other New York restaurants, a catering service, private label caviar and smoked salmon, five cookbooks, and the development of DBK kitchenware. Yet just as his heart has never strayed far from his native Lyon, neither does Boulud stray far from Daniel. "The kitchen at Daniel is my home," says Boulud. And when diners from New York and all over the world want a meal like no other, they often go to meet him there.

The depth and power of Les Pavots marries with the red-meat texture of the lamb and the overall richness of the dish. The wine's notes of cedar, cigar box, bay leaves, and blue oaks intermix with the rosemary in particular, but also with the fennel and cinnamon of the stew.

Grape phylloxera, a louse native to the Mississippi Valley, attacks the roots of grapevines. In the mid-19th century, infestations of this insect nearly wiped out the American wine industry and spread to Europe, destroying most of the vineyards there. Finally, it was discovered that a rootstock from Missouri had a natural resistance to the louse, and both European and American growers replanted their vineyards by grafting vines onto Missouri roots.

That didn't do away with grape phylloxera, however. In the late 1980s, the AXR-1 rootstock, thought to be resistant, proved vulnerable, and the louse forced the replanting of many California vineyards, including the first red wine grapes at Peter Michael Winery.

LAMB STEW WITH ROSEMARY AND ORANGE

6 Servings

---

4 to 6 tablespoons extra-virgin olive oil

2   pounds boneless lamb shoulder, cut into 1-inch chunks

     Salt and freshly ground pepper

1   large onion, cut into ½-inch wedges

4   small carrots, cut diagonally into ½-inch slices

2   large turnips, peeled and cut into ½-inch cubes (or 16 baby turnips, peeled and trimmed)

1   large celery root, peeled and cut into ½-inch cubes

1   medium fennel bulb, trimmed and cut into 6 wedges

3   cloves garlic, coarsely chopped

1   teaspoon finely chopped rosemary leaves

1   cinnamon stick (about 3 inches long)

¼   cup all-purpose flour

2   tablespoons tomato paste

1   teaspoon finely chopped flat-leaf parsley

     Freshly squeezed juice of 1 orange

½   cup dry white wine, such as Chardonnay or Sauvignon Blanc

5 to 6 cups water or unsalted chicken stock

4   plum tomatoes, peeled, seeded, and cut into ½-inch dice

½   teaspoon finely grated orange zest

1. *Sear lamb:* Heat 2 tablespoons of the oil in a 4-quart Dutch oven over high heat. Season the lamb with salt and pepper. Sear lamb chunks, about a fourth at a time, until golden brown on all sides. Remove meat as it browns and transfer to a plate. Add more oil to pan as needed.

2. *Cook vegetables:* Reduce heat to medium-high. Adding more oil to pan if needed, cook onion, carrots, turnips, celery root, fennel, garlic, rosemary, and cinnamon, stirring often, until vegetables are softened, 10 to 12 minutes. Season to taste with salt and pepper.

3. *Return lamb to pan:* Add seared lamb to vegetables and continue to cook and stir until mixture is hot, 6 to 8 minutes longer. Sprinkle flour over mixture, then cook and stir until all ingredients are coated with flour and flour begins to brown, about 5 minutes. Mix in tomato paste and parsley. Add orange juice and wine, stirring up

browned bits from pan. Cook, stirring occasionally, until liquid is reduced by half. Add enough water to almost cover the lamb and vegetables. Bring mixture to a boil, then mix in tomatoes and orange zest.

4. *Bake stew:* Cover pan and bake in a 300°F oven until lamb is very tender when pierced with a fork, 1 to 1¼ hours.

5. *Serve:* Divide meat and vegetables into wide shallow, bowls and spoon the sauce around them. Serve immediately.

Good fungus

To take advantage of the freshest ingredients, Chef Daniel Boulud has created entire menus of signature dishes for each of the four seasons. In the fall, he is often inspired by the fragrant, earthy white truffles of northern Italy. Every year from August to January, the hunt for white truffles centers around the city of Alba, in the mountainous Piedmont region. Hunters, called trifolau, use dogs trained to sniff out the delectable tubers that grow underground beneath certain oak trees.

In the markets of Alba, you can buy truffles whole, puréed, or blended with items such as olive oil, mayonnaise, or pasta. In the hands of Chef Boulud, you just might get braised turnips stuffed with pig's feet, and fall mushrooms with white truffle sauce.

JOHN CAMPBELL

John Campbell is often described as being a practitioner of "molecular gastronomy" or "scientific cooking." He doesn't dispute the label because he bases his cuisine on a thorough understanding of the chemical makeup of foodstuffs and knowing how those ingredients will react to heat, cold, and other ingredients. But he sees his methods as only a means to a higher end. "By understanding the cooking process logically, I can

throw away preconceived ideas and move my dishes forward without compromising on flavour," says Campbell. "But I never allow technical wizardry to deflect from the importance of taste." Indeed, as executive chef at The Vineyard at Stockcross, Sir Peter Michael's five-star hotel in Berkshire, Campbell claims his goal is to deliver the "wow" factor, presenting guests with a dining experience they have never had before. Based on the response of guests and critics alike, he is more than meeting his goal.

The Vineyard at Stockcross offers 49 luxurious
rooms and suites, from which guests may venture out to be pampered at
the spa, shoot a round at the challenging golf course, attend the races at
nearby Newbury, fish, shoot, or simply take in the large collection of
paintings and sculptures on display
in the hotel and on the surrounding
grounds. But diversions aside, The
Vineyard was always meant to be a
destination for world-class dining—
the hotel bills itself as "the restaurant
with room to stay"—and as a showcase for
its wine list of more than 2,000 selections.
The 60-seat dining room is decorated
in cream colors with an ironwork

balustrade of poppy leaves. A bank of windows overlooks *Fire and
Water*, a dramatic courtyard water feature by William Pye. Before
being seated, guests peruse the menu in the lounge, making selections
for a two- or three-course prix fixe dinner or choosing to sample a
broader range of the chef's expertise in the eight-course tasting menu.

Chef Campbell's cuisine is noted for combining unexpected ingredients, contrasting textures and temperatures, and his penchant for slow cooking at low temperatures. "Too often we crucify meat," says the chef. "Protein shrinks above 59° centigrade." One example of this technique is his fillet of beef with veal cheeks, pickled tongue, and beets, which roasts for close to an hour before emerging rare, tender, and delicious. One risotto of smoked haddock with frozen mustard sherbet shows the contrast of flavors and temperatures, while another with wild mushrooms features truffle jelly specially prepared to withstand the heat without melting. Other choices may include smoked organic salmon with spiced lentils, foie gras with fig and

apple chutney, homemade black pudding with apple panna cotta, saddle of rabbit with a risotto of peas and licorice, and an array of desserts often accompanied by exotic ice creams made with pepper, basil, beets, or parsnips.

Regardless of the choices, Campbell's kitchen delivers with scientific precision and consistency, and the formal but friendly waiters stand ready to offer tips on how best to enjoy the unique tastes and contrasts of the chef's offerings.

Given the proprietor, it is not surprising that The Vineyard's wine list is substantial. It's actually two lists: one features Peter Michael and other California wines from small, family-owned vineyards, many of which are available nowhere else in Europe; the international list has more than 1,000 selections including impressive verticals from the best of Burgundy and Bordeaux, as well as more than 300 selections from Italy.

With his meticulous and inventive cuisine as well as an acclaimed book called *Formulas for Flavour*, Chef Campbell's scientific approach to cooking is gaining ever wider acclaim. Yet he can scarcely imagine leaving The Vineyard at Stockcross. "It's the best place to offer true hospitality in this country, if not in Europe," says Campbell. "It's relaxed, it's informal, and it's a great formula because it's pure decadence." That is not a matter of science; that is purely a matter of taste.

Chef John Campbell writes, "The muscular aromas of the 2001 Belle-Côte match well and hold up to the meatiness of the oxtail and jus. The orange notes cut the denseness of the dish well, and the long finish allows the wine to carry with every mouthful."

In founding Peter Michael Winery, Pete and Maggie wanted to prove that California could produce wines of a style and quality that rivaled the very best of France, and to share that fact with Europe and the rest of the world. As they began to achieve their winemaking goals, they discovered that spreading the news was going to be equally challenging. Reliable channels for distributing limited production, high-quality California wines in Europe simply didn't exist.

Over the last few years, Pete and Maggie have taken the lead in bringing together California's finest family-owned estate wineries to act in concert to develop these channels. "It's hard work, and not nearly as much fun as making and tasting the wines," says Pete. "But it's the only way Europe will get a sense of what we're doing here."

ROAST TURBOT AND BRAISED OXTAIL

4 Servings

Oxtail

About ½ cup corn oil

1   carrot, cut into 1-inch pieces

1   leek (white and pale green parts only), rinsed and cut into 1-inch pieces

2   onions, coarsely chopped

1   meaty piece oxtail (about 2 lb.), trimmed of fat

3   cloves garlic

1   bay leaf

2   sprigs thyme

1   cup dry red wine

6   cups beef stock

Sauce

2   tablespoons (1 oz.) butter plus 4 tablespoons (2 oz.) cold butter

1   teaspoon chopped garlic

2   teaspoons chopped parsley

Salt and freshly ground pepper

Garnish

3   stalks salsify

Lemon juice

12   pearl onions

4   tablespoons (2 oz.) butter

½   cup small shiitake mushrooms, rinsed, patted dry, and cut in halves

4   cups spinach, rinsed and drained

2   cups hot mashed potatoes (see note)

Turbot

4   trimmed turbot or sea bass fillets (about 4 oz. each), rinsed and patted dry

Salt and freshly ground pepper

2 to 3 tablespoons corn oil

1. *Cook oxtail:* Add enough oil to cover bottom of an ovenproof sauté pan at least 12 inches in diameter. Heat oil over medium-high heat, then add carrot, leek, and onions. Cook, stirring often, until well browned. Spoon vegetables from pan into a bowl; set aside. Wipe out pan, then add more oil to cover pan bottom. Add oxtail and cook, turning as needed, until browned on all sides. Return vegetables to pan along with garlic, bay leaf, and thyme. Pour in wine, stirring to scrape up brown bits from pan, and bring to a boil. Add beef stock.

2. Cover pan tightly and transfer to a 325°F oven. Bake until meat is so tender it separates easily from bone, 3 to 3½ hours. Let oxtail stand until cool enough to touch, then remove meat from bones in long strips and set aside while preparing sauce.

3. *Make sauce:* Strain oxtail cooking liquid into a 3- to 4-quart pan, discarding solids. Bring to a boil over high heat, then adjust heat so liquid boils rapidly; cook, stirring occasionally, until reduced to about 1 cup. In a saucepan, melt the 2 tablespoons butter over medium heat. Add garlic and parsley; cook briefly until fragrant. Add reduced cooking liquid and bring to a boil. Whisk in the 4 tablespoons butter, 1 tablespoon at a time. Season to taste with salt and pepper, and keep sauce warm.

4. *Prepare garnish:* While sauce is reducing, peel salsify and cut into 2½-inch pieces. As salsify is cut, drop pieces into a saucepan of boiling water to which lemon juice has been added to prevent darkening. Cook until tender when pierced, about 7 minutes; drain well. Blanch onions by dropping into boiling water and cooking for 2 minutes. Drain and let cool, then cut off and discard root ends; slip off and discard skins. Heat butter in a 10-inch skillet over medium heat. Add onions and cook, turning as needed, until tender when pierced, 6 to 8 minutes. When onions are nearly done, add salsify and mushrooms to pan; cook and turn until golden.

5. *Cook fish:* Season turbot with salt and pepper. Heat oil in a wide skillet over medium-high heat. Add fish and cook for 2 minutes; carefully turn fish, then remove pan from heat and allow residual heat to cook fish on second sides.

6. *Serve:* Return pan with sauce to medium heat. Add strips of oxtail and let warm in sauce. Place spinach in a wide skillet over high heat, stirring just until wilted; remove from heat and quickly drain spinach. For each serving, spoon a portion of mashed potatoes into center of plate; top with a fourth of the spinach, and spoon onions and salsify around potatoes. Place a turbot fillet atop spinach, top with a strip of oxtail, and drizzle sauce around edge.

Note: For mashed potatoes, peel and quarter about 1¼ pounds Yukon Gold potatoes. Cook in boiling salted water until tender when pierced, about 15 minutes. Drain well, then mash until smooth with 1 to 2 tablespoons heavy cream, about 1 tablespoon butter, and salt and pepper to taste.

California in Europe

Many visitors to The Vineyard at Stockcross ask an obvious question: "Where's the vineyard?" The answer is that the vineyards are in California, and Pete and Maggie established their Berkshire hotel and restaurant as their first and best channel for sharing Peter Michael and other California wines with an audience in the UK and Europe.

The wine list at The Vineyard offers more than 800 selections from California, most of them from small, family-owned estate wineries, and many of the offerings available nowhere else in Europe. Still, this European outpost of California winemaking doesn't try to stack the deck. The Vineyard's list of European wines is just as formidable. After all, you can't have a friendly competition without a level playing field.

TOM COLICCHIO

Gramercy Tavern, the immensely popular New York restaurant opened in 1994 by Chef Tom Colicchio and his partner Danny Meyer, is more like two restaurants in one. The main and private dining rooms in the back offer contemporary American cuisine that is the rival in taste and sophistication of any restaurant in the world. The front room, or "tavern," takes no reservations and serves simpler fare such as poultry and fish prepared on a wood-burning grill. This combination of elegance and simplicity is very

much a part of Chef Colicchio's nature as well. A New Jersey native, he would just as soon talk fly-fishing as cooking. He tends to downplay the creativity of his task, attributing his inspiration to what the seasons are "saying" and what's on display at the Union Square Greenmarket. Yet his cuisine is famous for clean, bold flavors, the impeccable pairing of ingredients, and the French- and Italian-influenced touches he adds to American staples. His advice to amateur cooks may be to "trust your instincts and let fresh, seasonal ingredients dictate the way to go." But for anyone who has tasted his cooking, it is deliciously clear that not all instincts are created equal.

Gramercy Tavern is located in a converted industrial building on East 20th Street in Manhattan, not far from Gramercy Square. Rough-hewn beams, plank flooring and velvet curtains evoke the warmth and comforts of a bygone era. The

There is a three-course prix fixe menu offered at both lunch and dinner, as well as three chef's tasting menus. Given Colicchio's devotion to the freshest seasonal ingredients, it is not surprising that the menu is constantly changing. Still, dinner always begins with an

tavern's drop-in policy caters to neighborhood traffic and seems to lend the entire restaurant an air of relaxed conviviality. The mood is enhanced by the gracious service, a Meyer trademark. The waiters are friendly and knowledgeable but equally adept at turning to a more formal style should the occasion demand.

amuse-bouche or two and may include seafood specialties such as marinated hamachi with lemon-olive oil, roasted beets, and fresh herbs; lobster and artichoke salad with fresh herbs and basil oil; or salt-baked salmon with spring garlic, pea shoots, and rhubarb. The chef ably maintains the hearty traditions of tavern fare with specialties such as roasted lamb with fava beans and fingerling potatoes; roasted beef rib steak with braised short ribs, foie gras, and potato gratin; and braised veal cheeks with gnocchi and morels.

The wine list offers several hundred selections and, while it is deep in Burgundies, Bordeaux, and California wines, it has an eclectic reach that extends to rare bottlings from all over the world. To encourage guests to explore, an expansive list is offered by the glass and half glass. At the end of the meal, there is a fine selection of farmstead cheeses and desserts that range from a chocolate nib tart to dishes designed ingredient by ingredient around the freshest fruits of the season.

Tom Colicchio's philosophy of cooking is simple: the quality of the ingredients is everything. When the quality is there, all that is needed is the knowledge of time-honored techniques to prepare and combine those ingredients properly. When Gramercy Tavern was in the planning stages, it was his fondest wish to re-create the entire menu each day to take advantage of the best meat, fish, and produce available. That notion came to fruition later with the opening of his restaurant, Craft, where guests don't simply order meals, but select the dishes that will compose those meals. It is entirely in character that the chef claims that the best meal he has ever had was prepared with a group of friends, none of whom were professional cooks, and who used only what was on hand. "No one had any idea where we were headed (myself included), but we were hungry and liked good food, so we just let the ingredients dictate which path to take," says Colicchio. "Impromptu. Delicious."

The 2001 Pinot Noir Le Moulin Rouge provides a unique pairing with this rich stew. The wine's acidity contrasts with the plump flesh of the oysters while combining with the herbs (thyme, bay leaves) to bring lightness and freshness to the dish. The black truffles in the stock are enhanced by the wine's earthy notes of forest floor and black tea leaves.

OYSTER STEW WITH SALSIFY AND BLACK TRUFFLE

4 Servings

3	stalks salsify
	Lemon juice
1	leek
3	tablespoons peanut oil
1	small onion, diced
1	stalk celery, diced
	Salt and freshly ground pepper
1	sprig thyme
1	bay leaf
4½	cups chicken stock
24	small to medium oysters, such as Kumamoto, scrubbed
¼	cup Cognac
1	small to medium black truffle
2	tablespoons butter
	Chervil sprigs

Special equipment: An oyster knife

1. *Prepare salsify and leek:* Peel salsify and cut into 2-inch pieces. As salsify is cut, drop pieces into a bowl of cold water to which lemon juice has been added to prevent darkening. Trim and discard root end and dark green top from leek; remove tough outer leaves. Split leek in half lengthwise and rinse well, then cut into ½-inch slices.

2. *Cook vegetables:* Heat oil in a 2- to 3-quart sauté pan over medium heat. Add leek, onion, and celery; cook, stirring occasionally, until they begin to soften but not brown, 5 to 7 minutes. Season to taste with salt and pepper. Drain salsify and add to vegetable mixture with thyme and bay leaf. Pour in 4 cups of the chicken stock. Bring to a gentle boil and cook until salsify is tender when pierced, 8 to 10 minutes. Lift out 8 pieces of the salsify and set aside.

3. *Prepare oysters:* Shuck oysters (see note), reserving 12 of them for garnish. Add remaining 12 shucked oysters to soup and cook until edges curl, 8 to 10 minutes. Remove stew from heat; discard thyme and bay leaf. In a food processor or blender, whirl stew, about a third at a time, until puréed. Pour purée through a sieve into a large bowl, discarding solids. Let puréed stew stand until cooled to room temperature

4. *Make truffle liquor:* In a small pan, bring remaining ½ cup chicken stock to a simmer over medium-high heat. Add Cognac and truffle; cook until truffle is tender when pierced, 5 to 7 minutes. Remove truffle from liquor and let both truffle and liquor stand until cool.

5. *Prepare garnish:* Melt 1 tablespoon of the butter in a small nonstick skillet. Add reserved pieces of salsify and sauté until lightly browned. Slice truffle very thinly.

6. *Serve:* Pour puréed stew into saucepan and place over medium heat; mix in truffle liquor and remaining 1 tablespoon butter. Cook, stirring occasionally, until stew is steaming hot. Divide sautéed salsify, truffle slices, chervil sprigs, and remaining 12 oysters into 4 wide bowls. Ladle or pour hot soup over garnish in bowls. Serve immediately.

Note: To shuck an oyster, use a thick towel or a heavy glove to protect your hand, and hold the oyster firmly, cupped side down. Slide the tip of the oyster knife between the shells near the hinge, twisting and pushing the knife firmly into the opening to sever the hinge. Then slide the knife along the top shell and sever the muscle that holds it to the shell. Remove the top shell. Slide the knife under the meat to cut it away from the bottom shell.

It sounds delicious

Chef Tom Colicchio believes that ingredients are so paramount that they virtually dictate their preparation. This sometimes presents a challenge for the chef in creating menu descriptions (or, as he calls them, the "lyrics"). While a beef sirloin, a saddle of rabbit, and a loin of lamb may all be roasted, Colicchio will craft descriptions that avoid repetition and emphasize the unique preparations of accompanying ingredients. Sometimes a traditional preparation such as Bordelaise sauce will be redescribed simply for effect or to highlight how its elements pair with a particular dish.

Whether it's coining a term such as "tomato-onion jus" or differentiating among potatoes that are mashed, crushed, or puréed, there is clearly as much an art to making people want to order a delicious dish as there is to preparing it.

GARY DANKO

be featured in a book that celebrates the pairing of great cooking with great California wines. For in the 1980s, as more and more California wines were finding their way onto the lists of world class restaurants, Chef Danko was hard at work making sure world class cooking found its way to the California wine country. At the urging of Madeleine Kamman, his teacher and friend, Danko left the East Coast to join the food and wine program at Napa Valley's Beringer

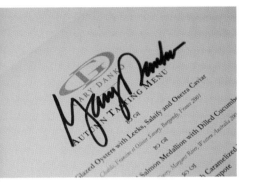

Vineyards and, in 1985, was made executive chef of the culinary center. When Beringer bought Chateau Souverain in Sonoma, Danko took over the restaurant, which was in sad disrepair, and within two years was receiving national attention for his cuisine. Part of his job was to travel the world talking about food and wine, but as he taught, he also studied. "It was an amazing education," says Danko. "You learn techniques from every culture and adapt them into your cooking." In 1991, he moved to San Francisco for what became a celebrated stay at the Ritz-Carlton and, in 1999, opened his own restaurant. But by that time, Danko's talent had helped to influence and forever change the wine country. It was no longer simply a wine tasting destination; it had become a dining destination as well.

Restaurant Gary Danko is on the north side of San Francisco, near Ghirardelli Square. Wood paneling, plantation shutters, and soft lighting give the two dining rooms a feeling of simple elegance. Guests are greeted with a series of small appetizers before ordering, a foretaste of the delights to come. Chef Danko

divides the menu into appetizers, seafood, meat and poultry, and cheese and desserts, offering several choices in each. Guests are allowed to mix and match dishes in three-, four-, or five-course prix fixe menus. With choices such as lobster salad with citrus segments, haricots verts, and mustard-tarragon vinaigrette; horseradish-crusted salmon medallion with dilled cucumbers; pan-roasted quail stuffed with wild mushrooms and foie gras; quinoa pilaf and pine nuts; and baked chocolate soufflé with two sauces, the menu is a tantalizing exercise in flexibility. In addition, a five-course tasting menu includes optional wine pairings.

The chef describes his cuisine as "lively, seasonal dishes prepared with a careful eye toward classical technique." His signature dishes of roast lobster, foie gras, and lamb loin are offered year-round with accompaniments reflecting the changes in season. But he does not embrace change for change's sake. In his mind, a perfectly prepared foie gras

can't be made any better by the addition of an unexpected ingredient. "People like familiarity, not necessarily things that are cutting edge," says Danko. "I do high-quality food simply." On the other hand, Danko has a love for the theater and a keen sense of the role of drama in a great restaurant. Whether it's planning each day's floral arrangements or artistic installations, making adjustments to the lighting, or selecting his waiter's suits, the chef's orchestration and attention to detail extend far beyond the kitchen to encompass every aspect of his guests' dining experience.

give advice, and coordinate effortlessly to make sure dishes arrive on time. The wine offerings are equally accommodating. The selections have grown from 600 at the time of the restaurant's opening to almost 2,000 at present, featuring a particularly strong showing in mature California wines, as well as white Burgundies, Bordeaux verticals, and red Rhônes.

Danko's culinary reputation and his demanding but even-keeled nature have combined to allow him to draw the cream of San Francisco's service profession to his restaurant. Dressed in dark suits and colorful ties, the friendly staff make guests comfortable,

Chef Danko likes to describe his restaurant as a "work-in-progress," but the fact remains that Restaurant Gary Danko opened in the summer of 1999 to instant public and critical acclaim, and continues to deliver one of the finest dining experiences in America. It isn't easy to do that. It requires meticulous planning, a

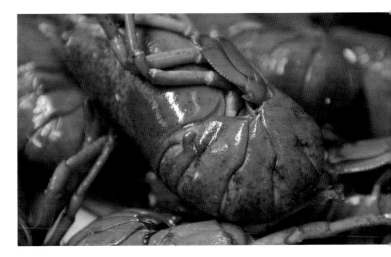

confident and unwavering vision, and the ability to deliver inventiveness and flair without being trendy or flashy. Though he has recently acquired property in the Napa Valley, where he grows some of his own produce and herbs, and talks of starting a cooking school, he still finds the challenge and drama of opening his restaurant each night to be completely fulfilling. "This is the only restaurant I've ever wanted," says Danko. " I'm home."

The 2001 Cuvée Indigène is an elegant choice for this dish because of its richness, its distinct silky texture, and its intense yet delicate and complex bouquet of orange blossom, dried apricot, ginger, and hazelnut. The wine's natural acidity complements the firm, delicate flesh of the lobster, while its long finish accompanies this dish all the way through.

ROAST LOBSTER WITH MOREL MUSHROOMS, ASPARAGUS, AND TARRAGON

6 Servings

Lobster and Sauce

3	live lobsters, about 1 pound each (see note)
	Olive oil
10	pencil-thin stalks asparagus, cut diagonally into 1-inch slices
8	ounces morel mushrooms
2	tablespoons (1 oz.) plus ½ cup (4 oz.) cold unsalted butter
½	cup dry white wine, such as Chardonnay or Sauvignon Blanc
¼	cup bottled clam juice
1	cup fish fumet (page 192)
1	shallot, finely minced
1	bay leaf
1	sprig thyme
¼	cup whipping cream
1	tablespoon chopped flat-leaf parsley
½	teaspoon chopped fresh tarragon
½	cup shelled edamame
1	teaspoon lemon juice
	Salt

Puréed Potatoes

1	pound large red or Yukon Gold potatoes
6	tablespoons (3 oz.) cold unsalted butter
	Kosher salt

1. *Cook lobsters:* Plunge lobsters, one at a time, into a large kettle of boiling water. Cook each for 4 minutes. As you remove lobsters, submerge in ice water and let stand until lobsters are cold. Drain well and pat dry. Cut each lobster in half lengthwise through the back. Remove meat from claws and tail; wipe shells clean. Replace half the tail meat in each tail half-shell; slip a claw into each half body carcass, as shown in photograph on page 97. Brush lightly with olive oil. Place filled shells in a single layer in a shallow pan, cover lightly, and refrigerate until ready to serve.

2. *Prepare asparagus and morels:* Blanch asparagus in boiling water for about 30 seconds. Drain well and transfer to a bowl of ice water until cold; drain well and set aside. Slice mushrooms in half lengthwise; rinse well to remove any grit, then pat dry. Melt 2 tablespoons of the butter in a wide skillet over medium-high heat; add mushrooms and cook, stirring occasionally, until lightly browned. Set aside.

3. *Make sauce:* In a nonreactive 1½- to 2-quart saucepan, combine wine, clam juice, fish fumet, shallot, bay leaf, and thyme. Bring to a boil over high heat, then reduce heat and boil gently until reduced by half. Mix in cream and return to a boil. Whisk in remaining ½ cup butter, 1 tablespoon at a time, until sauce is smoothly combined. Strain into a bowl, discarding solids. Mix in parsley, tarragon, asparagus, morels, edamame, and lemon juice; season to taste with salt. Place bowl over very hot (not boiling) water to keep sauce warm.

4. *Cook potatoes:* Peel potatoes, cut into quarters, and bring to a boil in a 2-quart pan with salted water to cover. Cook until potatoes are tender when pierced, about 15 minutes. Drain well, then put potatoes through a food mill or ricer; blend in butter and season to taste with salt.

5. *To serve:* Bake lobsters, uncovered, in a 350°F oven until heated through, about 10 minutes. For each serving, spoon a dollop of hot potatoes onto plate, top with a baked half lobster as arranged in step 1, and spoon warm sauce with asparagus, morels, and edamame around lobster.

Note: If you wish, you can purchase freshly cooked fresh lobsters from your seafood dealer. Begin preparation in step 1 by cutting each lobster in half, then proceeding as directed.

KEN FRANK

restaurant in the Napa Valley town of Rutherford, has spent more than two-thirds of his life in the kitchen. At 21, he was a celebrity chef in Los Angeles, the demanding and perfectionist enfant terrible of nouvelle cuisine. By the age of 24, he owned his own restaurant, the original La Toque on Sunset Boulevard, which he ran for 15 years. Then, after more than two decades of critical acclaim

and 100-hour weeks in the heady but fickle spotlight of LA, he relocated to Napa in 1998 and opened the new La Toque in a space leased from the Rancho Caymus Inn.

Says Frank, "I didn't want what I had to deal with in Los Angeles anymore—people who came in and wanted everything their way: a meal of grilled vegetables, with no sauce and no dessert and maybe a little diet soda." In a small northern California town, he doesn't have to worry about people coming to his restaurant to see and be seen; they come to eat. For a lifelong food fanatic, it was the ultimate lifestyle move.

What have become standards in today's finest restaurants—combining classic technique with the freshest local ingredients, constantly changing menus, and designing menus around a single ingredient such as truffles, garlic, or foie gras—Frank has been doing since the 1970s. He has always felt the importance of the food far outweighed the need for theatrics or eye-catching ambience, and that holds true at La Toque. The space feels like a French country inn, open and unadorned, with one wall dominated by a large stone fireplace. Flower arrangements by his wife, Sherylle, provide splashes of color, but the overall impression is still one of a clean canvas upon which the chef will perform his artistry. The waiters, many of whom followed Frank from Los Angeles, are skilled, knowledgeable, and very accommodating. They seem as happy to be there as he is.

The menu is a five-course prix fixe offering, providing guests with a couple of choices for each course. Selections have included New England spotted skate wing with Zante currants, seared artisan foie gras with fresh corn polenta and chanterelles, oxtail ragout with Reggiano flan, and wild Atlantic striped bass with lobster Cabernet sauce. Controlling the size of the offering and changing it weekly allows the chef to pursue his passion for innovation. There are Mediterranean influences in some dishes and Japanese in others, born of his own love for sushi.

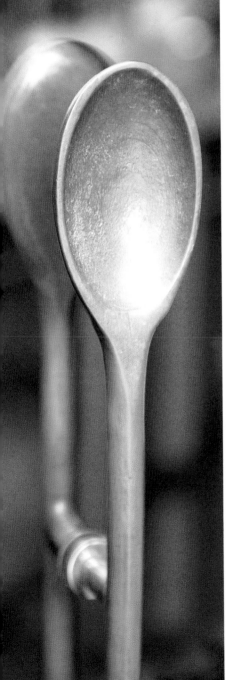

Each year, in season, the chef also offers his renowned Truffle Menus. They begin in November with the white truffles from Alba, then shift to black truffles in January as they appear on the scene. Last year, drought decimated the supply and quality of white truffles, so Frank simply cancelled the menu. In short, he cooks what he wants, when he wants. "Moving to Napa Valley was the smartest thing I've ever done," says Frank. "La Toque is doing fine here. I couldn't have this kind of restaurant just anywhere."

The wine list already has over 900 selections, featuring the best of France, Napa, and Sonoma, but it continues to grow quickly as Frank explores the possibilities of his wine country locale. He refers to La Toque as a "wine restaurant," a place where exploring and experimenting with great food and wine is not just possible, but encouraged. In fact, the optional four-glass wine pairing offered with the dinner menu provides ample support for this philosophy. The choices are bold and eclectic but unerringly successful.

One way of looking at Ken Frank's move to Rutherford is that he was fleeing the nonstop pressures of the Los Angeles restaurant scene. But he wasn't running away from anything. Rather, he was moving toward what, for him, had always mattered most—the food. It was the move of a man mature and confident in his talent, one who is clear about the environment required to let that talent shine. And if that means that people have to plan a little more and travel a little farther to enjoy one of his meals, that's fine with him. Ken Frank knows that sometimes you have to go the distance to find just what you want.

The 2001 Les Pavots has rich,

opulent tannins that carry well through

each bite, while its impressively long

finish accompanies the thick and deep

reduction sauce.

Punching the cap

When making red wine, the "cap" is a solid mass of grape skins and pips (seeds) that floats to the top of the fermenting vessel during fermentation. "Punching down" simply means breaking up the cap and pushing it back down into the wine. This step introduces oxygen to the yeast cells to promote fermentation while ensuring that color, flavor, and tannins are added to the wine.

At Peter Michael Winery, the cap is punched down in the making of the Pinot Noir, Le Moulin Rouge. However, a pumping over process is used in the fermentation of Les Pavots.

NIMAN RANCH RIB ROAST WITH ITS OWN HACHIS PARMENTIER

8 Servings

1	boneless rib-eye roast of beef (about 6 lb.)
2	tablespoons vegetable oil
1	medium-size onion, cut into ½-inch chunks
1	carrot, cut into ½-inch chunks
2	stalks celery, cut into ½-inch chunks
	Salt and freshly ground pepper
1	bottle (750 ml) Cabernet Sauvignon (see note)
4	cups veal stock
6	large Yukon Gold potatoes (about 2½ lb. total)
6	tablespoons (3 oz.) plus about 2 tablespoons (1 oz.) unsalted butter
3	ounces foie gras
1	clove garlic, peeled and cut in half
3	packages (6 oz. each) baby spinach

1. *Prepare beef:* Trim the cap or lifter muscle from the roast and set it aside. Tie the remaining eye of beef securely with string at 1½-inch intervals; cover and refrigerate. Cut the cap meat into 2-inch squares, and set aside.

2. *Begin cooking hachis parmentier:* Heat oil in a 10-inch braising pan over medium heat; add onion, carrot, and celery. Cook, stirring occasionally, until vegetables begin to brown. Season cap meat with salt and pepper. Add to onion mixture; cook and stir until browned, about 5 minutes longer. Spoon off and discard excess fat from pan. Pour in most of the wine, scraping up brown bits from pan. Then add veal stock. Bring mixture to a boil, reduce heat to low, and cook, partially covered, until the meat is very tender and sauce is reduced by about half and has a rich flavor, 3 to 4 hours. During cooking, occasionally skim and discard fat and foam from top of mixture.

3. *Bake potatoes:* About 45 minutes before hachis mixture is ready, bake potatoes in a 425°F oven until tender when pierced. Let stand until cool enough to handle.

4. *Prepare foie gras butter:* In food processor, combine the 6 tablespoons butter and foie gras; whirl until puréed. Then press through a fine strainer into a bowl. Set mixture aside.

5. *Roast beef:* Let roast stand at room temperature for about 45 minutes, then season with salt and pepper. Quickly sear in a large sauté pan over high heat, turning to brown all sides. Then transfer pan with roast to a 500°F oven and roast until a roasting thermometer inserted in center registers 135°F, 12 to 14 minutes. Remove from oven, cover loosely with foil, and let rest for 15 minutes.

6. *Complete hachis parmentier:* With a slotted spoon, lift the chopped cap meat from the cooking liquid, reserving meat and liquid separately. Chop meat finely. Cut potatoes in halves and scoop potato out of skins. With a fork, mash potatoes in a bowl with chopped meat, half of the foie gras butter, and additional butter and salt and pepper to taste. Keep mixture warm.

7. *Finish sauce:* Strain liquid, discarding remaining solids. Return liquid to pan and boil gently, if necessary, to thicken. Swirl in remaining foie gras butter.

8. *Cook spinach:* Rub a wide skillet with garlic, then melt about 1 tablespoon of the remaining butter in pan over medium-high heat. Stir in spinach and cook just until wilted. Season to taste with salt.

9. *Serve:* Place roast on a board and cut into 8 slices. On each plate, spoon an oval of the hachis parmentier, then a bed of hot spinach in front of it; top with a slice of beef and spoon sauce around the meat.

Note: Chef Frank advises, "Save a little of the wine for inspiration and cook with the rest."

Tracing the hat

Ken Frank's restaurant, La Toque, is named in honor of the tall white hat traditionally worn by chefs. But how did the tradition begin? The most prevalent theory dates back to the days of the Byzantine Empire. As invading barbarians approached, chefs, as well as other artisans, sought refuge in monasteries. In order to fit in, they began to wear the tall black hats worn by the Greek Orthodox priests who lived there. What started out as "camouflage" soon became tradition, and, over the centuries, the color shifted to white as a way of communicating cleanliness and sanitation.

By the way, the head chef's hat is traditionally the tallest so that he or she is easier to spot from across a crowded kitchen.

SUZANNE GOIN

In Los Angeles, a town known for A-lists,

the latest fads, and turning the wildest fantasies into reality, Chef Suzanne Goin

has bucked convention, becoming a sensation by presenting a cuisine and

dining experience that are described as "honest" and "unpretentious" and

"stylishly simple." The venue for these impressions is Lucques, the restaurant

Goin opened with business partner Caroline

Styne in September 1998. Their shared

vision was simple, to create a restaurant that they themselves would like to

go to. Drawing on their combined experience—Goin honed her skills at

restaurants such as Al Forno, Chez Panisse, Arpege, Olives, and Campanile

while Styne founded Basically Baked, Inc., and managed Jones Hollywood—

they knew just how to execute that vision.

Lucques is on Melrose Avenue in West Hollywood, in a structure that once served as the carriage house for silent screen star Harold Lloyd. The space features brick walls, exposed beams, a central fireplace ringed with sofas, and a light-filled patio where guests can dine under the stars. "We knew the feel we wanted the place to have," says Goin. "Homey and comfortable and magical—a place to live for a few hours."

Chef Goin serves what she calls her "Mediterranean-influenced comfort food" for both lunch and dinner, with a special menu for Sunday supper. Guests are greeted with a banette of bread, roasted almonds, fleur de sel, and lucques, the juicy green olives from France's Languedoc that give the restaurant its name. The menu, a single sheet fastened to a board with a rubber band, offers a half-dozen starters, 8 to 10 main courses, and extras in straightforward, easy-to-read language. The understated elegance of the surroundings and the congenial service create a relaxed atmosphere where the colors and flavors of Goin's creations seem all the more vibrant in their purity and clarity. Some of her specialties include foie gras terrine with sautéed pears; rack of lamb with flageolet gratin, roasted radicchio, and tapenade; cured pork chop with black-eyed peas, pearl onions, and cavolo nero (Tuscan black cabbage); and roasted snapper with saffron rice, preserved lemons, and green olives. For those dining late or alone, the bar menu features items such as steak frites, spaghetti carbonara, and an omelet with soft herbs and Cantal cheese.

The menu changes with the seasons as Goin pursues her goal of using only local and organic produce, wild fish, and naturally raised meats. Alice Waters considers Goin to be one of the most eco-conscious chefs in the country, and Goin, in turn, cites Waters's influence. "Chez Panisse helped me focus on clean flavors," says Goin. "I learned to let the ingredients be the stars."

Styne is a warm presence in the dining room, where she helps the staff see to the comfort of the guests while also serving as sommelier. The wine list is eclectic and constantly evolving as Styne shares her discovery of new wines and producers.

"I'd just like Lucques to go on and on and stop being new," Goin says, "and become like Campanile and Spago—one of the city's long-lived restaurants." Indeed, Lucques has the feel of a restaurant that has been around much longer than it has, certain in its style and confident in its cuisine and presentation. Lucques makes its guests feel so comfortable because its proprietors are so comfortable in themselves. Perhaps it is because, in a city where so many people come from afar to try to re-create themselves, Goin and Styne are native Angelenos. By contrast, Goin traveled the world to discover, develop, and refine her palate. And now, she is sharing that palate with the world in a place and in a way that feels just like home.

"The richness of the wine balanced with its minerality brought to mind one of my favorite dishes inspired by an old Andre Soltner recipe...the smokiness of the bacon with the sweet corn and fatty fish seemed a lively complement," says Suzanne Goin.

Green

For Pete and Maggie, protecting the environment on the ranch is a cornerstone of their farming and winemaking philosophy. Over the years, they've planted thousands of trees to help preserve the soil and watershed. The vineyards have been planned from the outset to be worked with sustainable winemaking practices, including fish-friendly farming that limits runoff into streams, land conservation, erosion control, and integrated pest management.

"We try to keep things as natural as possible," says Pete. *"Our commitment to 'terroir' and to our family legacy demands it."*

WILD SALMON "À LA LUTÈCE" WITH SWEET CORN AND GREEN CABBAGE

6 Servings

Sauce

½	cup (4 oz.) unsalted butter
2	tablespoons red wine vinegar
½	teaspoon kosher salt
¼	cup finely diced onion
2	tablespoons coarsely chopped parsley
½	lemon, cut lengthwise into 2 wedges

Batter

	1 to 1½ cups whole milk
3	ounces slab bacon, coarsely chopped
2	large eggs
2¼	cups medium-fine fresh bread crumbs
2	tablespoons coarsely chopped parsley

Vegetables

3	tablespoons unsalted butter
2	spring onions or green onions, white part and 1 inch of the green part only, thinly sliced diagonally
2	teaspoons fresh thyme leaves
5	ounces slab bacon, cut into 1- by ¼-inch lardons ¼ inch thick, and cooked until crisp
1½	cups fresh corn kernels (from 3 ears of corn)
½	head green cabbage, cored and thinly sliced
3	tablespoons vegetable stock, chicken stock, or water
	Kosher salt and freshly ground pepper

Salmon

6	boneless, skinless wild salmon fillets (about 5 oz. each), rinsed and patted dry
	Kosher salt and freshly ground pepper
	1 to 2 tablespoons vegetable oil

1. *Begin the sauce:* In a small sauté pan or skillet, melt the butter over medium-high heat. Continue to cook, shaking pan occasionally, until butter is a deep brown and has a toasty aroma, 3 to 4 minutes. Pour into a small saucepan and let stand until cool, about 5 minutes. Stir in vinegar and salt, then set aside.

2. *Make the batter:* In a small saucepan, combine 1 cup of the milk and bacon. Bring to a boil over medium-high heat. Remove from heat and let stand until slightly cooled, about 5 minutes. Pour mixture into food processor or blender and whirl to purée bacon. Add eggs and whirl again. Pour mixture into a large bowl; mix in bread crumbs and parsley. Set aside while cooking vegetables.

3. *Cook vegetables:* In a large sauté pan, melt butter over medium heat. Add onions, thyme, and lardons of bacon; cook just until onions are translucent, about 3 minutes. Then add corn and cook, stirring occasionally, until corn is about half cooked, about 3 minutes. Add cabbage and stock; continue cooking until cabbage is wilted, about 2 minutes longer. Season to taste with salt and pepper. Transfer to an ovenproof platter and keep warm in a 250°F oven while preparing salmon.

4. *Cook salmon:* Season salmon with salt and pepper. Dip each fillet into the batter, patting batter onto the fish to coat generously (if batter is too thick, stir in up to ½ cup more milk).

5. Heat 2 wide, heavy skillets over medium-high heat until hot but not smoking (or cook salmon, 3 fillets at a time, in a single pan). Add 1 tablespoon of the oil to each pan. Place salmon in hot pans; if some of the batter slides off, spoon more over the salmon and spread it evenly after the fish is in the pans.

6. Reduce heat to low and cook until golden brown on both sides, turning carefully once, 6 to 8 minutes total. Remove platter of vegetables from oven and arrange salmon over vegetables.

7. *Complete the sauce:* While the fish is cooking, place pan of brown butter over medium heat and bring to a low simmer. Stir in diced onion and cook until it begins to soften, about 2 minutes. Remove from heat and add parsley and the juice of 1 of the lemon wedges.

8. *Serve:* Spoon sauce equally over each serving of salmon, then squeeze remaining lemon wedge over all.

And green

Suzanne Goin is an eco-conscious chef—a trait she attributes to the time she spent working with Alice Waters. Chef Goin uses organic ingredients for 80 percent of her dishes. Line-caught fish, hormone-free meat, and artisanal cheeses are staples in her recipes. She also returns her compost to local farmers, sends her leftover grease to a local company to make soap, and recycles mustard tubs for use as kitchen storage containers.

"Alice inspires you to call up the city of Los Angeles and fight about recycling," Goin says, "even when every ounce of your energy is directed toward getting dinner out."

J. JOHO

He is still very much the native son of Alsace, the French region where he grew up

and which still inspires much of his classic French cuisine. Yet he is equally dedicated

to his adopted city of Chicago and uses almost exclusively American ingredients in

his dishes. He is an avid entrepreneur with

restaurants in Chicago and Las Vegas, but likes

nothing better than cooking at home with his

young daughter. His recipes, too, reflect this drive to embrace, even celebrate, contrast.

"I like to blend noble ingredients like caviar and foie gras with simple ingredients like

potatoes and turnips," says Joho. "The union of simple and noble makes for unique

flavor combinations."

Joho's flagship restaurant, Everest, which opened in 1986, also strikes this perfect balance between elegance and comfort. Perched on the 40th floor of the Chicago Stock Exchange building, Everest is reached by private elevator and offers

panoramic views of Chicago. Yet the highly descriptive menu and the friendly and helpful waiters never let this exclusive setting feel intimidating. There is also an emphasis on flexibility. Guests can select a multicourse degustation menu, which displays a broad

range of Chef Joho's creativity. But they can also order à la carte or from the pretheater menu, a quick, elegant three-course repast for those on the way to the nearby theaters, opera, or symphony.

Each guest is welcomed with an amuse-bouche that embodies Chef Joho's philosophy of marrying the noble and the simple—a silver spoon bearing a cauliflower fondant topped with caviar and sprigs of dill. Dishes such as roasted chestnut soup with duck confit, risotto inlaid with black trumpet mushrooms and topped with quail, venison with wild huckleberries, wilted cabbage and knoepfle (the Alsatian

version of spaetzle) and New York State foie gras roasted with *suri ruebe*, Colmar style, appear with Chef Joho's signature attention to detail, creative presentation, and devoted allegiance to the unique Alsatian gastronomy.

Also in keeping with his heritage, the chef is a master of bringing fruit and pastry together to heavenly effect. Dessert selections include a pear charlotte in a crust of sourdough brioche with cinnamon, a napoleon of apples with caramel sauce, and a pineapple strudel baked with caramelized macadamia nuts and served with coconut ice cream and mango coulis.

Not surprisingly, of the more than 1,500 selections on Everest's well-rounded wine list, close to 350 of the offerings are from Alsace, easily the best collection in the hemisphere. With a lengthy late-harvest list including many of the sweet Sélection de Grains Nobles, Chef Joho gives the selection of a wine for dessert the same sort of prominence and interest as for any other part of the meal.

Perhaps, after all, it is inaccurate to speak of J. Joho in terms of contrast, for those contrasts in his heritage, nature, and experience seem to have found such perfect integration. How else to explain a restaurant as

elegant as Everest, steeped in classic French procedures, that still manages to exude Midwestern comfort and friendliness. How else to explain a style of cuisine where the exotic ingredients and flawless technique rival those of any chef in the world while at the same time delivering the flavors, textures, and earthy satisfaction of French home cooking. "Top chefs taste food all day long, every day," says Joho. "It takes many years to really develop your palate. It's not something that can be learned from a book or improvised." Chef Joho has clearly developed his palate. He is cooking food that he loves, providing fond echoes of the place of his birth, and he is sharing it with a graciousness and style that are felt by every guest who walks through his door.

The richness and zest (natural high acidity) of the 2001 L'Après-Midi provide a superb complement to foie gras. Medium bodied with a layered finish, the wine matches each melt-in-your-mouth bite, while its hints of white truffle pair with the truffle oil used for seasoning.

In a field sit the huge

golden balls of "Brontosaurus
Eggs." Along pathways rest giant
nails in rock, ceramic, and
bronze. Waves of Water flow
from the contours of black granite.
A walk through the grounds of
Sugarloaf Ranch reveals Pete's
lifelong love of sculpture, a
passion that led him to establish
an artist-in-residence program
at the ranch. The works on
the ranch were left behind by
grateful participants.

"The pieces do make some
interesting additions to the
scenery," says Pete in an
understatement!

NAPOLEON OF ALSACE CABBAGE AND FOIE GRAS

4 Servings

Cabbage

10	ounces double-smoked bacon, finely chopped
1	small onion, finely chopped
1	clove garlic, minced
1	bay leaf
1	sprig thyme
1	teaspoon coriander seeds
1	teaspoon caraway seeds
½	medium-size head green cabbage, cored and shredded
2	cups dry white wine
1	large egg, lightly beaten
¼	cup whipping cream

Pinch freshly ground nutmeg

Truffle Vinaigrette

1	black truffle, chopped
5	tablespoons peanut oil
1	tablespoon white wine vinegar

Salt and freshly ground pepper

Napoleons

1	package (about 1 lb.) puff pastry
	About 8 ounces foie gras, sliced into 4 medallions
1½	tablespoons butter
4	quail eggs
1	bunch mâche, rinsed, drained, and chilled

Special equipment: Parchment paper

1. *Prepare cabbage:* In a large, heavy, ovenproof skillet over medium heat, combine half of the bacon with onion and garlic; cook, stirring occasionally, until onion is soft. While onion is cooking, tie bay leaf, thyme, coriander seeds, and caraway seeds securely in a square of cheesecloth to make a bouquet garni. Add to pan along with cabbage and wine. Bring to a boil, then cover and transfer pan to a

325°F oven. Bake for 35 minutes. Remove from oven, discard bouquet garni, and transfer cabbage mixture to a bowl. Cool, then cover and refrigerate for at least 8 hours or until next day.

2. *Prepare vinaigrette:* In blender, combine truffle, oil, and vinegar. Whirl until puréed; pour into a medium-size bowl and season to taste with salt and pepper. Set dressing aside.

3. *Bake cabbage:* Drain cabbage and measure 1 cup (save any remaining cabbage for another use). In a bowl, combine the 1 cup cabbage with remaining 5 ounces chopped bacon, egg, cream, and nutmeg; mix well. Spread mixture in a shallow 2-quart baking dish. Bake in a 275°F oven until set, about 30 minutes. Set baked cabbage aside.

4. *Bake puff pastry:* On a floured surface, roll puff pastry out paper-thin. Cut into 3-inch rounds (see note) and arrange on a parchment paper–lined baking sheet; prick each pastry with a fork in several places. Bake in a 350°F oven until golden brown, 8 to 10 minutes. Set aside just until cool.

5. *Begin assembling napoleons:* Spoon a circle of cabbage on each of 8 puff pastry rounds. On each plate, carefully stack 2 cabbage-topped pastries. Then cover each with a plain puff pastry round.

6. *Sear foie gras:* Preheat a heavy skillet over high heat. Season foie gras with salt and pepper to taste. Working quickly, sear each medallion of foie gras just until brown, a few seconds on each side.

7. *Serve:* Place a seared foie gras medallion on top of each puff pastry stack. Melt butter in a small nonstick skillet over medium heat. Add quail eggs, one at a time, and cook just until set, about 45 seconds. As each egg cooks, place it atop foie gras on one of the stacks. Sprinkle with freshly ground pepper. Stir vinaigrette to blend and lightly mix in mâche. Lift out sprigs of mâche and garnish each plate. Drizzle remaining vinaigrette around stacks and serve at once.

Note: You need 12 baked puff pastry rounds, but bake any extras in order to allow for breakage as you assemble the fragile pastries.

The art of forms

In Chef J Joho's restaurant, Everest, a small bronze statue sits at the center of every table. The bronzes are the work of Ivo Soldini, a versatile Swiss artist who sculpts, draws, paints, and creates monumental works for public spaces around the world. Joho is obviously an admirer of Soldini's works and appreciates the beauty they bring to his restaurant. But there is more to it than that. "Sculpting and cooking are both three-dimensional art forms," says Joho. "You begin with the raw materials of nature and seek to create something that elevates and inspires while remaining in harmony with the essence of those materials."

Of course, the best part about Chef Joho's own sculptures is that you get to eat them.

THOMAS KELLER

Chef Thomas Keller's The French Laundry in Yountville, California, has

been acclaimed as one of the best restaurants in America. The success of

The French Laundry is based almost as much on how you are prepared for

the dining experience as it is on the meal

itself. The peaceful small-town atmosphere

of Yountville exudes a sense of relaxation, the verdant beauty of the

surrounding wine country awakens the senses, and the simple remoteness of

the location seems to add focus and purpose. There is really only one

reason to be there: to have one of the best meals of your life.

The century-old fieldstone building where the 62-seat restaurant is located was indeed once a working steam laundry. But with its surrounding gardens, climbing roses, and simple but elegant interior, it now feels more like a country cottage. The staff enhances the feeling of relaxed comfort. They are so

meticulously trained and the pacing is so flawless that it almost seems effortless.

When it comes to the food, Keller adds to the comfort level with his celebrated culinary wit. The menu features dishes such as "macaroni and cheese" and "coffee and donuts." That the first turns out to be orzo in coral oil with mascarpone topped with lobster and a parmesan chip, and the second a cup of cappuccino semifreddo surrounded by small cinnamon pastries only adds to the disarming effect. "Coming to a restaurant like this can be intimidating. And that's the last thing I want," says Keller. "I don't want people to come here afraid, like it's some kind of temple of gastronomy. It's just a restaurant. Coffee and doughnuts on the menu should make you smile. It gets everyone laughing and in a good mood. Anything I can do to relieve the pressure of eating in a restaurant, I want to do."

If the diner's choice is one of the chef's renowned tasting menus, expect to spend more than three pressure-free hours enjoying Keller's unique ability to balance the rustic and refined—a cauliflower panna cotta topped with glazed oysters and osetra caviar—or even seeming polar opposites such as butter-poached Maine lobster with bone marrow, shiitake mushrooms, a scallion salad, and Bordelaise sauce. These creations are ably supported by a 41-page wine list featuring many unusual and limited-production offerings from the wineries nearby.

The French Laundry's outward projection of comfort and relaxation does not come without a price. Behind the scenes, all is discipline and control. The chef is notorious for his fanatical attention to detail. The kitchen, prep, and storage areas are surgically clean and precisely organized. After almost 30 years in kitchens, Keller is still a constant presence, overseeing the almost 1,000 courses that are prepared and presented on an average night.

Thomas Keller's passion and dedication are not devoted exclusively to the experience of his patrons. He has an almost mystical reverence for the food with which he works. A simple example is that he insists that his fish always be put on ice in "swimming" position, to cause them less stress. "At some point you either have to learn or be taught the importance of the food that we eat," says Keller. "It's not about thanking God or anybody; that's an individual thing. But it is about understanding the relationship between you and the food. And how that relationship has to be nurtured."

For anyone who has had the good fortune to have dined at The French Laundry, Thomas Keller's relationship with the food is a delicious and lasting memory.

The 2001 *L'Après-Midi* uniquely complements this dessert by contrasting with the overall creaminess of the dish while underlining the acidity of the rhubarb and the reduced balsamic vinegar. The wine's fruit aromas and high natural acidic structure bring crispness and freshness to the dish. *L'Après-Midi* joins with the ice cream to refresh the palate while savoring this rich ending to the meal.

The term "terroir" dates to the Middle Ages, when it is first found in the writings of the Cistercian monks of Burgundy. The monks literally tasted the soil to identify the ideal locations to plant their vines. Past experience and "tastings" had taught them what soil and mineral combinations imbued the grapes with the best flavor.

There is no word from Peter Michael winemaker, Luc Morlet, on what exactly Mount St. Helena tastes like. But we're willing to bet he knows.

SEBASTIEN'S RHUBARB TART

8 Servings

Rhubarb Filling and Compote

5   stalks rhubarb (about 1¼ lb.)

3   tablespoons plus ¼ cup granulated sugar

1   recipe Pâte Sucrée (page 191)

¼   cup water

½   cup grenadine syrup

Alsatian Cream

1   large egg

⅓   cup granulated sugar

2   tablespoons whole milk

2   tablespoons whipping cream

½   cup almond flour (see note)

3   tablespoons butter, browned and cooled to room temperature

Almond Streusel

6   tablespoons (3 oz.) cold butter, diced

6   tablespoons granulated sugar

¼   teaspoon kosher salt

¾   cup all-purpose flour

¾   cup almond flour

Garnish

½   cup balsamic vinegar

   Powdered sugar

1   pint vanilla ice cream

Special equipment: 8-inch-square tart pan with removable bottom

1. *Prepare the rhubarb for the filling:* At least 8 hours before making tart, peel 3 stalks of the rhubarb and slice diagonally about ¾ inch thick. Place in a nonreactive container, sprinkle with the 3 tablespoons sugar, cover, and let stand at room temperature for at least 8 hours or overnight.

2. *Bake pastry:* On a lightly floured surface, roll out Pâte Sucrée to a 10-inch square. Carefully fit into an 8-inch-square tart pan with a removable bottom, fitting pastry against bottom and sides of pan. Trim pastry even with top edge of pan. Cover pastry with foil or parchment paper and partially fill with uncooked beans or rice. Bake in a 425°F oven for 10 minutes; lift off foil and continue to bake until light golden brown, about 5 minutes longer. Place pan on a rack to cool.

3. *Strain rhubarb:* Pour prepared rhubarb into a strainer and let stand while pastry is baking. Discard liquid.

4. *Make Alsatian Cream:* Combine egg and the ⅓ cup sugar in a bowl; beat or whisk until mixture is pale. Whisk in, in order: milk, cream, almond flour, and browned butter; mixing well after each addition.

5. *Fill and bake pastry:* Pour enough of the cream mixture into baked pastry shell to make a thin layer. Then fill with strained rhubarb. Pour remaining cream mixture evenly over rhubarb. Bake in a 350°F oven until filling is set and top is lightly browned, 30 to 35 minutes.

6. *Make Almond Streusel:* While tart is baking, in a bowl combine diced butter, the 6 tablespoons sugar, salt, flour, and almond flour. With your fingers or two knives, blend mixture until it resembles coarse sand.

7. *Complete tart:* Reserving about ⅓ cup of the streusel mixture for garnish, sprinkle remaining streusel evenly over the top of the tart. Return tart to a 450°F oven and bake just until streusel is golden, 3 to 5 minutes. Let tart cool on a rack. Reduce oven temperature to 350°F. Sprinkle remaining ⅓ cup streusel into a shallow pan and bake until lightly toasted, 3 to 5 minutes.

8. *Prepare rhubarb compote:* Finely dice the remaining 2 stalks rhubarb. In a 1½ - to

2-quart nonreactive pan, combine grenadine, water, and remaining ¼ cup sugar. Bring to a boil over high heat, then reduce heat to medium and cook for about 3 minutes. Stir in rhubarb and continue to cook until rhubarb is just tender and liquid is syrupy, about 5 minutes. Let stand until cool (compote thickens as it cools).

9. *Make balsamic reduction:* Pour balsamic vinegar into a small pan. Bring to a boil, then reduce heat and boil gently until vinegar is reduced by half and has a syrupy consistency, 2 to 3 minutes. Watch carefully so that vinegar does not become too thick.

10. *Serve:* Sprinkle tart lightly with powdered sugar. Carefully remove tart from pan and cut in half lengthwise, then cut each half crosswise into 4 small rectangles. For each serving, place a rectangle of tart at one side of plate. Sprinkle a small spoonful of the toasted streusel next to it, then scatter a few bits of streusel in a line across the bottom of the plate at a right angle to the tart. Spoon a strip of rhubarb compote parallel to tart at other side of plate. Then drizzle one stripe of balsamic reduction to the right of the tart and another to the left of the compote. Place a scoop of ice cream on top of the streusel next to the tart.

Note: Look for almond flour (also called almond meal) in a store that specializes in natural foods. It is made from skinless, blanched almonds that have been finely ground.

PATRICK O'CONNELL

offering world-class dining, the finest restaurants in the United States tend to be found in large cities. A few exceptions to this rule have come upon the scene in the last decade, but one—The Inn at Little Washington—has been going strong for over a quarter of a century. In 1978, Chef Patrick O'Connell and his partner, Reinhardt Lynch, opened a restaurant in a converted garage in the small hamlet of Washington, Virginia, located about 70 miles west of Washington, D.C. In the 26 years since, the self-taught O'Connell has evolved his cooking from traditional

French recipes to a highly creative cuisine featuring native Virginia ingredients, Indian and Japanese influences, and classical technique. The garage has been transformed into an elegant country inn and guesthouse with nine rooms and five suites; the recently added Mayor's House and beautifully refurbished Farmhouse offer more private accommodations. The interior design has become the lifetime project of Joyce Evans, a London set designer, who selects the lush fabrics, antiques, and William Morris wall coverings, and furnishes the rooms down to the last bit of bric-a-brac. And guiding this evolution throughout has been an unerring sense of taste, a flair for theatricality, and the clear conviction on the part of O'Connell and Lynch that The Inn at Little Washington is more than their life's work: it is their masterpiece.

Like the rest of The Inn, the 100-seat dining room manages to strike a balance between sumptuous décor and inviting comfort. Velvet banquettes are strewn with pillows, and rose-colored silk lampshades hover above each table, casting a warm glow. Two Chef's Tables are available in the kitchen, where diners can watch the staff at work at a 16-foot brass and bottle green Vulcan stove while Gregorian chants play over the sound system.

Under the guidance of Lynch, the service is formal but gracious, and guests are greeted with a tray of tidbits such as a miniature BLT, a salmon pinwheel, and a sliver of fried parmesan. The seven-course prix fixe dinner allows guests to choose from a number of dishes, and a ten-course tasting menu and a vegetarian tasting menu are available as well. The presence of rabbit, rockfish, shad roe, and Virginia country ham reflect Chef O'Connell's passion for the bounty of the local countryside. Some of The Inn's specialties include boudin blanc on sauerkraut braised in Virginia Riesling, seared duck foie gras on polenta with country ham and huckleberries, local rabbit braised in apple cider with wild mushrooms and a yellow grits soufflé, and rockfish roasted with white wine, clams, shrimp, mussels, and black olives on toasted couscous.

The wine list has over 900 selections drawing on a cellar with close to 16,000 bottles. The finest vintages from Burgundy, Bordeaux, and California are represented and, as might be expected, the very best from Virginia's rapidly developing wineries as well. Dessert selections include rosemary-scented crème brûlée, and "my grandmother's rhubarb pizza" with buttermilk ice cream. Or, if one is not enough, The Inn's specialty is a sampling called Seven Deadly Sins.

In 1749, George Washington surveyed and laid out the town that was to become Little Washington. No doubt, he assumed the small hamlet would act as a center of trade for surrounding farms, and it has. What he couldn't have foreseen is that two centuries later Little Washington would also become the place where two men would seek to redefine luxury, comfort, and hospitality. Patrick O'Connell and Reinhardt Lynch want a visit with them to be nothing less than transformative, a temporary idyll where guests' every need is anticipated while they are gently enfolded in the unique taste and whimsy of their hosts. In short, The Inn at Little Washington is not really a country inn; it's another world entirely. "What's so appealing is that this is intended to be a total artwork," says O'Connell, "and as with any artwork, it has to have a soul. The more of yourself you put into it, the better it will be. There is no stopping point."

The 2001 Pinot Noir' Le Moulin Rouge has a voluptuous palate, full body and stunning concentration that complement the rich, tender slices of lamb, while the wine's acidity combines with the arugula and mint leaf to bring lightness and freshness. The concentrated bouquet of strawberries, black cherries, raspberries, mint, black tea leaves, lilacs, and forest floor also interact with the refined flavors of the dish.

Everyone at Peter Michael Winery is pleased to share the steep slopes of Mount St. Helena with nesting peregrine falcons, classified as an endangered species in both Canada and the United States.

These birds of prey feature blue-black plumage on their backs and pale, cream-colored feathers barred with black on their bellies and under their wings. Peregrines prey on other birds, striking them in midair after diving from above at speeds of up to 200 miles per hour, making them the fastest birds in the world.

Mountain-bred, rare, and spectacular, the peregrines make a fitting, if unofficial, mascot for the winery.

CARPACCIO OF BABY LAMB ON ARUGULA WITH ROASTED GARLIC SAUCE AND TABBOULEH

6 Servings

Carpaccio

2	boneless lamb loins (12 to 15 oz. total), trimmed of fat
	Salt and freshly ground pepper
1	tablespoon dried tarragon
1	tablespoon dried thyme
1	tablespoon dried oregano
1	tablespoon dried basil
1 to 2	tablespoons olive oil

Roasted Garlic Sauce

½	cup olive oil
1	sprig rosemary
½	cup mayonnaise
2	tablespoons roasted garlic (see note)
1	teaspoon lemon juice
1	teaspoon chopped fresh rosemary

Tabbouleh

2	tablespoons bulgur wheat
¼	cup boiling water
1	teaspoon chopped fresh mint
1	teaspoon chopped fresh parsley
1	teaspoon chopped shallot
1	tablespoon olive oil
1	teaspoon peeled, seeded, and chopped tomato
½	teaspoon minced garlic
1	tablespoon lemon juice

Garnish

2	bunches arugula, rinsed, drained, and chilled
3	sprigs mint
2	teaspoons drained capers

1. *Prepare carpaccio:* Season lamb generously with salt and pepper. In a small bowl, mix tarragon, thyme, oregano, and basil. Pat herb mixture over lamb to coat completely. Heat a large nonstick skillet over high heat; meanwhile, drizzle oil over lamb. One at a time, place each lamb loin in hot skillet and roll to sear exterior, allowing only the herbs to brown. As each loin is seared, remove it from the pan and let stand at room temperature until cooled.

2. *Freeze lamb loins:* Enclose each cooled lamb loin tightly in plastic wrap, squeezing each into a smooth cylinder. Freeze until solid, about 2 hours.

3. *Make sauce:* In a small pan, heat oil and rosemary sprig over medium heat until rosemary begins to darken. Remove and discard rosemary; let oil cool to room temperature. In a bowl, whisk together mayonnaise and garlic. Whisk cooled oil into garlic-mayonnaise mixture, pouring oil in a thin stream, until well combined. Whisk in lemon juice. Pour through a strainer set over a bowl to remove any garlic solids. Stir in chopped rosemary. Transfer sauce to a squeeze bottle with a narrow tip; refrigerate until ready to serve.

4. *Prepare tabbouleh:* Place bulgur in a small bowl; pour on the boiling water. Let stand until bulgur is softened, about 20 minutes. Drain, discarding any excess water. To bulgur add mint, parsley, shallot, oil, tomato, garlic, and lemon juice. Season to taste with salt and pepper.

5. *Serve:* Remove lamb from freezer and let stand for about 5 minutes. Arrange arugula in clusters around each of 3 large plates (each plate will be shared by two people). Squeeze the sauce around inside edge of each plate in a lacy looping pattern. Slice the lamb very thinly and arrange a third of it in overlapping circles on each plate; the lamb will be thawed by the time it reaches the table. Place a third of the tabbouleh in center of lamb on each plate; garnish each with a mint sprig. Decorate each plate with a few capers.

Note: To roast garlic, place 1 or more large, whole, unpeeled bulbs of garlic in an oiled baking pan. Bake, uncovered, in a 325°F oven until tender when pierced, about 1 hour. To use the garlic, pluck out each clove and squeeze the roast garlic into a small bowl.

Favorite spots

In her interior design of the Inn at Little Washington, London-based set designer Joyce Evans has made every room eclectic and unique. But there is a recurring motif—in a word, spots. This is in honor of The Inn's official Dalmatian mascots. The first, DeSoto, was given to Patrick and Reinhardt by the staff in 1987.

A year later, Rose arrived, and her regal presence graced The Inn until 2001. Her obituary ran in the Style section of the Washington Post. A second Rose and her companion, JoBe, are now in residence.

From stuffed Dalmatian toys in the rooms to an array of spotted items in the gift shop to the Dalmatian-spotted trousers worn by the kitchen staff, Patrick and Reinhardt's beloved pets have more than made their mark on The Inn at Little Washington.

MICHEL RICHARD

Michel Richard is an artist.

He paints and designs furniture, and, as with most artists, he begins his

creations with detailed sketches of his vision for the finished work. The fact

that Richard also happens to be one of the world's most celebrated chefs does

not alter his practice. As each new recipe develops in his fertile imagination,

he creates a sketch that he and his staff will

use as a blueprint for the presentation of

the finished dish. Presiding over his cele-

brated Washington, D.C., restaurant, Citronelle, Chef Richard combines the

precision and attention to detail he learned in his early training as a pastry

chef in France. His artistic flair and playful sense of humor bring forth a cuisine

that is at once deliciously inventive, visually striking, and whimsically

entertaining. "I want my own style," says Richard. "I don't want to copy what

other people are doing."

Chef Richard first achieved fame in 1986 with the opening of Citrus in Los Angeles. Other branches followed in Santa Barbara, San Francisco, Philadelphia, Baltimore, and D.C. In 1998, the chef decided to concentrate his focus on Citronelle, and moved his family to the nation's capital. His attentions paid off, and Citronelle has been one of Washington's most sought-after reservations ever since.

Citronelle is located in The Latham Hotel in Georgetown. Diners enter through the bar and lounge, then descend a short flight of steps to the main dining area, which consists of two rooms decorated in light wood and warm, golden fabrics. The front room offers views of the glassed-in exhibition kitchen (a special Chef's Table is available behind the glass). The back room features a "mood wall," which changes color constantly, and, behind more glass, the 8,000-bottle wine cellar.

Guests are greeted with an amuse-bouche and can then select dishes for a three-course prix fixe dinner or choose the tasting menu, the Promenade Gourmande. The menu changes with the season's freshest ingredients, but favorites include foie gras three ways and squab presented with a quickly sautéed "minute-steak" breast and a potato-crusted leg confit. Chef Richard's playful imagination is apparent throughout. He has re-created the hamburger out of lobster and bay scallops, and "breakfast at Citronelle" is a dessert of sweet brioche toast, chocolate puff pastry "bacon," and an "egg" of cream cheese topped with an apricot and ginger purée. "Sushi d'ici" (the French for "here" is a play on D.C.) is inspired by sushi shapes and colors but made from the likes of veal and foie gras on a rice look-alike of potato or macaroni. The breathtaking carpaccio mosaic is an arrangement of circular shavings of tuna, eel roulade, lobster, yellowtail, venison, and yellow bell peppers that looks like raindrops striking a Technicolor pool. The chef's creations are ably supported by the 300 labels on the wine list, a selection that is particularly strong in white Burgundy, wines from Alsace, and rare California bottlings.

Michel Richard is a man who has found his perfect balance. He manages to indulge his whimsical nature without in any way diminishing the seriousness of his art. He is devoted to classic French technique but is in love with America and the unique ingredients it brings to his cuisine. He is often in the dining area of Citronelle greeting and conversing with guests, yet rarely does a plate go out without receiving his rigorous inspection. His creations are fanciful and entertaining, but they require the utmost of care and precision in their preparation. His imagination is as ever-changing as the colors on his mood wall, but his restaurant is a model of consistency. Of course, it takes an incredible amount of effort and discipline to strike this balance, but Chef Richard would rather keep that to himself. After all, artists must have their secrets.

The 2001 L'Après-Midi ably complements this scallop dish. The wine's crispness (high natural acidity), along with aromas of lime peel, citrus oil, gooseberry, and sweet pear juice, contrast with the soft, white flesh of the scallops, bringing freshness to the tomatoes- and onion-based sauce and accompany the light vinaigrette of the beets.

Part of the fun
of enjoying great wines is in trying to describe the way they taste. Wine experts have developed a lexicon that ranges from comparisons to other fruits and flowers to more arcane descriptors such as tobacco, cedar box, old leather, smoke, liquid mineral, tea leaves, and forest floor. While these terms may sometimes be a source of puzzlement and even amusement, the fact that the effort is so diligently made is a tribute to the unique depth, complexity, and variety in the flavors of wine.

Put it this way: when was the last time you heard someone break down the taste components of a New York steak?

SCALLOP PORCUPINE

6 Servings

Sauce

1	tablespoon olive oil
2	yellow onions, chopped
4	tomatoes, chopped
1	small beet, peeled and diced
1	clove garlic, thinly sliced
1	teaspoon red wine vinegar
	Salt and freshly ground pepper

Beets

2	medium-sized beets, scrubbed
2	tablespoons olive oil
4	sprigs thyme
½	teaspoon red wine vinegar

Scallops

	About half of a 16-ounce package kataifi (shredded phyllo dough)
⅓	cup all-purpose flour
1	large egg, at room temperature
1	tablespoon water
	Salt and freshly ground pepper
6	large scallops, rinsed and patted dry
	About 1 quart vegetable oil for deep-frying

Special equipment: Parchment paper

1. *Make sauce:* Heat oil in a 10-inch skillet over medium heat. Add onions and cook, stirring occasionally, until softened; add tomatoes, diced beet, and garlic. Reduce heat and simmer until vegetables are tender and liquid is reduced by half, about 10 minutes. Pour mixture through a sieve into a bowl, pressing down to remove all the liquid. Discard solids. To sauce add the 1 teaspoon vinegar, then season to taste with salt and pepper. Set sauce aside.

2. *Bake beets:* Place each beet on a 12-inch square of aluminum foil. Drizzle ½ tablespoon of the olive oil over each beet, then add 2 thyme sprigs. Fold foil into a packet to enclose each beet. Place packets on a baking sheet in a 350°F oven and bake until beets are tender when pierced, 45 minutes to 1 hour. Carefully open packets to let steam escape. Set beets aside to cool.

3. *Prepare baked beets:* Carefully peel beets, then trim edges so each beet is square. Cut into ¼-inch cubes. Place in a bowl and mix lightly with remaining 1 tablespoon olive oil, the ½ teaspoon vinegar, and salt and pepper to taste.

4. *Prepare scallops for frying:* Line a large baking sheet with parchment paper. Pull the kataifi from the bag and, holding it over a bowl, cut into 4-inch pieces. Separate the pieces into threads. Place the kataifi on a large plate and the flour on another. In a bowl, beat egg with water until blended; season to taste with salt and pepper. One at a time, dip scallops into flour until coated, patting off excess flour. Holding scallop with tongs, dip into the egg mixture to coat completely. Then lower scallop into kataifi, turning it to coat generously. Place the kataifi-coated scallop in the palm of your hand and press the kataifi firmly over the scallop to make a 2½-inch-diameter sphere. As each scallop is covered with the kataifi, place it on the parchment-lined baking sheet.

5. *Cook scallops:* Pour oil to a depth of 2 inches into a wok or wide saucepan and heat to 350°F on a frying thermometer. Line a large baking sheet with paper towels. One at a time, hold prepared scallop with tongs and dip into the oil; when the bottom layer of kataifi has set, immerse the scallop completely in the oil. Cook until golden brown on all sides, about 3 minutes. Carefully lift out and drain on paper towels. Repeat with remaining scallops.

6. *Serve:* Spoon a little of the sauce into the center of each plate. Cover sauce with a spoonful of the diced beets. Then place a hot, cooked scallop atop beets. Serve immediately.

Note: Leftover kataifi can be refrigerated or frozen in a tightly closed plastic bag for another use.

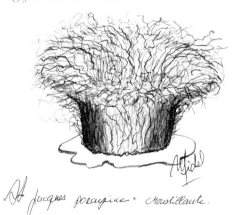

St Jacques porcupine + croustillante.

ERIC RIPERT

It seems that Eric Ripert was destined

to cook fish. As a child in Antibes, France, he watched as his grandmother

prepared seafood fresh from the fishing boats. As a young chef, the trend

continued. "For some reason, everywhere I worked I spent most of my

time at the fish station," says Ripert. By

the time he joined the New York restaurant

Le Bernardin, in 1991, he was more than ready to make this world-famous

temple to seafood his home.

The brother and sister team of Gilbert and Maguy La Coze opened Le Bernardin in 1986 after creating a sensation in their Paris restaurant by applying classic French principles to cooking fish. Le Bernardin was an immediate and lasting success, but when Gilbert died suddenly, in 1994, Maguy asked the 29-year-old Ripert to meet the challenge of maintaining that legacy. Ten years later, the two are now partners in the venture and Le Bernardin's star has never burned brighter.

There is irony in saying Ripert was born to cook fish because the exquisite preparations at Le Bernardin often mean barely cooking it, or not cooking it at all. He claims the first phase in developing his cuisine was simply learning the best way to prepare each variety of fish or shellfish to take maximum advantage of its unique texture and often subtle, delicate flavor. The second phase was to create dishes that made the fish the star. Chef Ripert sees himself as having entered a third phase. "Now I try to find the perfect harmony between all the ingredients. I still want to make the fish the star of the plate, but the fish should also enhance the vegetable and the sauce."

Le Bernardin is located in the Equitable Building on West 51st Street between 6th and 7th Avenues in Manhattan. In the main dining room, deep blue carpeting and walls combine with the warm color of the teak ceiling, paneling, and banquettes to create a feeling of comfortable elegance. The waiters work with an efficiency and discretion that has made Le Bernardin a favorite for high-powered business lunches as well as romantic dinners.

Lunch guests are offered several choices on a two-course prix fixe menu. At dinner, there is a three-course prix fixe menu as well as two six-course tasting menus with optional wine pairings. The menu is organized by style of preparation. Under "Almost Raw" are dishes such as thinly sliced geoduck clam with wasabi-lime dressing, urchin and scallop marinated with lime and extra-virgin olive oil ceviche style. "Barely Touched" offers, among others, juniper-crusted tuna on peppers and eggplant compote with Meyer lemon and olive oil emulsion; and ravioli of Argentinean shrimp and wild mushrooms with foie gras-truffle sauce. Selections under "Lightly Cooked" include poached skate wing with lemon brown butter, tangy carrot-lemon broth, and butternut squash; and crispy Chinese-spiced black bass in a Peking duck bouillon scented with chanterelles and enoki mushrooms. The wine list is deep in white wines, featuring the finest wines of Burgandy and Bordeaux, as well as an extensive collection of the best California bottlings.

Chef Ripert is known as an enthusiastic but patient teacher of his art, and turnover in his kitchen is low. Still, he tests the texture of every piece of fish and tastes every sauce before it's delivered to the table. "A conductor doesn't play all of the instruments, but he is responsible for how they sound," says Ripert. On the other hand, he is not completely comfortable in the role of celebrity chef, for he clearly feels that his status has as much to do with his patrons as himself. "I like to please people," says Ripert. "You don't create a dish to keep it; you create a dish to give to somebody. If somebody says it was horrible, I will not sleep at night. I missed what I am supposed to do." Those sound like the words of someone doing what he's destined to do.

The 2001 L'Après-Midi is a non-malolactic wine, and its full natural acidity marries seamlessly with the raw tuna, while its aromas of lime peel, citrus oil, gooseberry, and pineapple create an intense bouquet to accompany the freshness of the dish.

Hands

One of the innovations at Peter Michael Winery is the berry-sorting table for red wine grapes. After exiting the destemmer, the grapes are spread on the belt of the gently sloping table as ten experts, including winemaker Luc Morlet, line the sides. Then, in a ballet of discerning hands and eyes, bits of stem and damaged fruit are removed until only the most perfect berries move on to the fermenters. "It takes a lot of concentration because you have to be both thorough and fast," says Morlet. "But the improved overall quality of the fruit makes it worth it."

HAMACHI TARTARE

4 Servings

Vinaigrette

¼   cup lime juice

1½   teaspoons wasabi powder

       Pinch togarashi powder
       (optional)

½   cup canola oil

1½   tablespoons ginger oil

Tartare

4   hamachi fillets (3 oz. each),
       skinned and cut into ¼-inch cubes

½   cup wasabi tobiko

1   tablespoon ginger oil

1   tablespoon thinly slivered
       cilantro leaves

1   tablespoon chopped chives

1   tablespoon canola oil

1   tablespoon lemon juice

1   tablespoon lime juice

About 1 tablespoon wasabi powder

Fine sea salt

Freshly ground white pepper

Garnish

Cilantro sprouts

Special equipment:
2-inch-diameter ring mold

1. *Make vinaigrette:* In a small bowl, combine lime juice, wasabi powder, and togarashi powder (if used). Whisking constantly, slowly drizzle canola oil and ginger oil into the lime juice mixture until well blended. Set vinaigrette aside.

2. *Prepare tartare:* In a bowl, combine hamachi, ¼ cup of the wasabi tobiko, ginger oil, slivered cilantro, chives, canola oil, lemon juice, and lime juice. Mix lightly, then season to taste with wasabi powder, sea salt, and white pepper.

3. *Serve:* For each serving, place a 2-inch ring on a cold appetizer plate and fill about three-fourths full with the tartare mixture. Spoon 1 tablespoon of the remaining wasabi tobiko atop each serving of tartare. Whisk vinaigrette to blend well, then drizzle about 1 tablespoon vinaigrette around the tartare.

Carefully lift off the ring mold and top each serving with cilantro sprouts. Serve immediately.

Note: Togarashi powder, also known as ichimi, is a powdered red Japanese chili. Look for it, as well as ginger oil, in an Asian market. For wasabi tobiko (a fish roe seasoned with wasabi) and hamachi, seek out a fish market that specializes in sushi fish.

And hearts

One of Eric Ripert's close friends is a heart surgeon. The chef has observed his friend at work in his operating theater and finds the precision and coordination of a crack surgical team to be very similar to that of professional chefs working together in a busy kitchen. In fact, the surgeon has even spent a few nights working in Ripert's kitchen. "For all our training and rational technique, there are points in time when instinct must take over," says Ripert. "That's true whether you're a doctor or a chef."

We still think that most people would prefer a reservation at Chef Ripert's table rather than at that of his friend.

GUENTER SEEGER

Guenter Seeger is a chef who has always done things his own way, confident that the clarity of his vision and the quality of his cuisine would find their own appreciative audience. He has never been wrong. After receiving formal training in Switzerland, Chef Seeger returned to his native Germany in 1977 to open his first restaurant, named Hoheneck, in Pforzheim, the gateway to the Black Forest. His re-creations of traditional German dishes  using French techniques and exotic ingredients puzzled the locals but quickly drew acclaim from patrons and critics all over Europe. In 1985, he moved to Atlanta and transformed The Dining Room at the Ritz-Carlton Buckhead into one of the nation's best restaurants. At the same time, his passion for the freshest and finest ingredients led him to become a driving force in the founding of the Georgia Organic Growers Association. Finally, in 1997, he opened Seeger's, a restaurant that was designed from top to bottom to be the ultimate expression of doing it his way. Naturally, the restaurant has been a runaway hit.

Chef Seeger's "way" is all about striking a balance between catering to the whims of his guests and fulfilling his vision of what their experience should be. Seeger's, the restaurant, is in a Craftsman-style house in Buckhead, an upscale section of Atlanta, and it offers the atmosphere and comfort of dining in a home. Yet the restaurant's kitchen actually takes up more space than the main dining room. The waiters exude Southern-style charm and hospitality, but are outfitted in sober dark suits and reverently present dishes from silver trays. The menu's language is so straightforward and free of flourish that it almost seems an understatement, but it

reflects Seeger's emphasis on focus and clarity. "My food is always in movement, determined by the day, the season, the year," says the chef. "It can come out sometimes as, say, a little German, Japanese, or Italian, but I don't mix things up. And I don't put 20 things on a plate, with all this chichi all over. I put one thing on a plate, and that's it."

In keeping with the chef's philosophy, Seeger's is a study in minimal elegance. Red carpeting, yellow leather banquettes, and a cherry wood staircase lend warmth and richness, but the simplicity of the décor is clearly designed to make the food the center of attention. Flower arrangements add splashes of color and provide further testimony to the chef's attention to detail. "I use only organically grown flowers," says Seeger. "I can tell the difference. They have a more natural look, brighter colors, and more energy." Along with the main dining room, there are the Cellar Room downstairs for

special wine dinners and the Chef's Table where portholes provide a view into the kitchen to watch the chef at work. There are a five-course prix fixe dinner, which allows guests to choose from a number of selections for each course, and a set eight-course grand tasting menu. In season, Chef Seeger also creates a special black and white truffle menu.

While the menu changes constantly, some specialties include Champagne and sea urchin soup; a rich tuna tartare studded with

peanuts and resting on gazpacho; squab breast in five spices with Lakota squash and vanilla baked fig; steamed halibut pavé with marinated pepper, organic egg, and a sweet pepper reduction; and desserts such as an apple beignet with Tahitian vanilla sauce and apple sorbet. Regardless of the choice, Seeger's cooking is renowned for its balanced ingredients, focused flavors, and the ability to be at

once startlingly original and deeply satisfying. Meanwhile, the wine list offers close to 1,000 choices drawing from a cellar of more than 8,000 bottles. It is particularly strong in Burgundies, Rhônes, rare California offerings, and—befitting Seeger's heritage—wines from Germany and Alsace.

Guenter Seeger placed his restaurant in a house out of a sense of tradition. "This is where restaurants were born and where they should be," says Seeger. "People used to open their houses to people traveling on horse to come eat and rest. In Germany, we call this a gasthaus (guesthouse)." But it is equally clear that Seeger wanted a place to feel at home. From his expansive and beloved kitchen to the chandelier made by his grandfather that hangs in the lounge to his steadfast refusal to offer valet parking to the disciplined virtuosity of his cooking, the chef is unquestionably the master of his domain. He welcomes guests graciously and provides for them lavishly, but he will do things his way. "We love to make people happy," says the chef. "But people have to adapt to what we do." When Guenter Seeger is cooking, adapting is a deliciously easy thing to do.

The 1997 Les Pavots, year by year, exhibits more of its "wild" side (cassis, leather, earthy notes, forest floor), marrying beautifully with the wild mushrooms and the pronounced yet delicate flavor of the venison. The wine's round, silky tannins also highlight the subtle sweetness of the roasted and caramelized apples.

One of the recent innovations at Peter Michael Winery has been the addition of a vertical press. The purpose of this press is to squeeze the pomace (the pulpy mass of red wine grape skins) after it has been gently removed from the fermenters. The slow autofiltering squeeze allows the press wine to flow directly into barrels by gravity.

While the pomace may yield only a few barrels of wine, the winemaking team may find that they provide an integral flavor component in creating the over-all Les Pavots blend. Says Winemaker Luc Morlet, "You never know where that crucial piece of the puzzle is going to come from." In other words, press on.

VENISON LOIN POACHED IN RED WINE WITH ROAST CÈPES AND BAKED GEORGIA APPLES

6 Servings

Baked Apples

4   large Gala apples, peeled, cored, and thinly sliced

3   tablespoons turbinado sugar (raw sugar crystals)

     Salt

Venison

2   cups dry red wine, such as Cabernet Sauvignon

1   cup red port

1   venison loin (3 to 4 lb.)

Sauce

1¼   cups Fortified Venison Stock (page 191)

6   tablespoons venison poaching liquid

1   tablespoon cold butter

     Salt and freshly ground pepper

Cèpes

¼   cup peanut oil

2   sprigs rosemary

3   cèpes, each 3 to 4 inches in diameter, rinsed gently and patted dry

     Extra-virgin olive oil

     Salt and pepper

1. *Bake apples:* In a covered 2- to 3-quart casserole, make layers of apple slices, sprinkling each layer with a little of the sugar and the middle layer with a pinch of salt. Bake, covered, in a 250°F oven until apples are very soft and sugar is caramelized, 4 to 5 hours. Let stand at room temperature while cooking venison.

2. *Poach venison:* In a deep pan wide enough to hold the venison, combine red wine and port. Bring to a boil over high heat, then reduce heat to medium-high and boil gently for 5 minutes. Reduce heat to low and gently lower venison into liquid.

Cook, uncovered, until meat in center is medium-rare (cut to test), 12 to 15 minutes. Lift out meat, place on a carving board, and let rest for 2 to 3 minutes. Reserve poaching liquid.

3. *Make sauce:* In a 1- to 1½-quart saucepan, combine venison stock and the 6 tablespoons poaching liquid. Bring to a simmer over medium heat. Add butter and cook, swirling pan to mix in butter, until all the butter is melted and blended into the sauce. Remove from heat and season to taste with salt and pepper.

4. *Fry rosemary and grill cèpes:* In a small skillet, heat peanut oil to 325°F on a deep-frying thermometer. Add rosemary and fry just until fragrant, 20 to 25 seconds. Remove from oil and drain on a paper towel.

5. Cut each cèpe in half lengthwise and lightly coat with olive oil, then season to taste with salt and pepper. Heat a ridged grill pan over medium-high heat until a drop of water sizzles on the grill. Place cèpes on grill pan, cut sides down. Cook, carefully turning once, until cèpes are tender when pierced and browned on both sides, 6 to 8 minutes in all. Remove from pan and keep warm.

6. *Serve:* Cut venison into 12 slices. For each serving, overlap 2 slices venison on a warm plate. Add a spoonful of the baked apples and a grilled cèpe half. Strip fried rosemary leaves from stems, and sprinkle leaves over cèpes to garnish. Drizzle sauce around venison.

Kitchen made

When Guenter Seeger designed his restaurant, he devoted two-thirds of the 5,000-square-foot space to the kitchen. Climate control keeps the area at a constant 68°F for optimum cooking. Windows and sage-colored tile walls provide a backdrop, a sound system pipes in music, and Seeger and his staff communicate through radio headsets. The centerpiece of the kitchen is a 6- by 9-foot red-enameled Morice stove with polished brass and stainless steel fittings. Custom-built in France at Seeger's direction, the stove has two gas flattops on each side, four gas ovens, two open gas burners, an open flame grill and two electric warming ovens.

Says the chef about his kitchen, "It's my living room."

JOACHIM SPLICHAL

designed Walt Disney Concert Hall is reinvigorating the physical and cultural

landscape of downtown Los Angeles. It also seems to have reenergized one of

the city's culinary legends, Chef Joachim Splichal, whose flagship restaurant,

Patina, has moved from its original Melrose Avenue location to become the

centerpiece of the dining facilities at the new

Music Center. This is not to say that Splichal

has been biding his time. Along with his wife, Christine, he oversees a series

of restaurants and catering activities throughout Southern California, including

cafes in many of the area's major cultural venues. But with the move of

Patina, he has shifted his focus from the operations side and is back in the

kitchen with a vengeance.

He has been working side by side with Executive Chef Theo Schoenegger to make sure the new location both lives up to and transcends the original. "Patina has a lot of baggage," says Splichal. "Expectations are high. It's important for me to pick up a pan, to help." Since first arriving in Los Angeles in 1981, "picking up a pan" for Splichal has meant combining highly constructed, classically French cuisine with unexpected ingredients and uniquely contrasting flavors and textures. Foie gras and truffles are stars in his kitchen, but so, too, are potatoes, simple beans, and long-braised meats. Scallops wrapped in crisp potato, or lobster on a bed of white bean purée flecked with ham hock, are examples of the chef's mixing of the haute and the humble to magical effect.

The original Patina, which opened in 1989, was set in a converted apartment house. The new space is far more open, with a high, undulating wood ceiling and solid walnut paneling. To accommodate concert and theater patrons, Patina offers a special preperformance prix fixe menu and a comfortable lounge area serviced by the chef's favorite new touch, a caviar cart. "It will be a mix of American, Russian, and Iranian caviar, great for after theater with Champagne," says Splichal.

The dinner menu is elegant but understated, presenting the selections as a simple listing of ingredients. Along with an array of first and second courses offered à la carte, the prix fixe Ocean Menu features dishes such as sautéed blue prawns on creamy polenta, celery root emulsion, and black truffles; and black sea bass with zucchini flowers, cockles, and saffron risotto. In the autumn, the Wild Game Menu is a Patina signature. This year it includes seared loin of hare with chestnut spaetzle, pear and cranberry relish, and bitter chocolate sauce; and a slow-roasted venison loin with a foie gras–porcini–polenta napoleon and huckleberry relish.

Patina has always been noted for its service, with the staff moving seamlessly from providing helpful suggestions to quietly attending to the theater of tableside preparation. The wine list is equally versatile, with more than 1,600

particularly deep choices from California, Burgundy, Bordeaux, and the Rhône Valley.

The new Patina clearly bears the stamp of the

master—his skill, his passion, his whimsical imagination, and his commitment to the culture of Los Angeles. While many chefs of his stature have sought to take their image national, Splichal has remained focused on Southern California. His drive to transform the cuisine for the area's museums and concert venues was personal. "We are a Los Angeles company," says Splichal. "We live here. Our children grow up here. We use the museums like other people." And now, the restaurant that is closest to his heart has moved to the concert hall that is the epi-center of Los Angeles's cultural renaissance. There's no doubt that Joachim Splichal will provide pitch-perfect accompaniment.

The natural acidity of the 2001 La Carrière creates a splendid contrast with the softness of the white flesh of the scallops, while its mineral elements enhance the iodine notes of the caviar. In turn, the wine's hints of butter and toasted bread are a tempting match for the buttery scallops and homemade chips.

Bearing fruit

Over the past several growing seasons, a local black bear has developed a taste for Peter Michael grapes. He has managed to thwart any attempts to keep him out of the vineyards, and his nose for both the quality and the ripeness of the fruit often leads him to visit a block the night before the picking crew arrives. The bear's forays are a source of amused frustration for the winemaking team. After all, who's going to stop him.

"He probably eats a ton and a half of fruit a season," says Winemaker Luc Morlet. Now, that's what we'd call an allocation.

TOWER OF POTATO CHIPS, SCALLOPS, AND CAVIAR

6 Servings

- ¼ cup (2 oz.) unsalted butter, melted
- Salt and freshly ground white pepper
- 2 large Idaho russet potatoes (10 to 14 oz. each)
- 6 ounces (about ¾ cup) crème fraîche
- 2 tablespoons finely chopped chives
- 6 large scallops, rinsed and patted dry
- 3 ounces sevruga caviar
- 1 small head frisée, rinsed and chilled

Special equipment: Parchment paper

1. *Prepare potatoes:* Line a large baking sheet with parchment paper and brush with some of the butter; sprinkle with salt and pepper. Peel potatoes. With a vegetable slicer, cut each potato into thin slices. Then trim slices into 24 circles slightly larger than the diameter of the scallops. Place potato slices in a single layer on prepared parchment. Brush with more of the butter, then cover with another sheet of parchment, and a second baking sheet to keep potatoes flat.

2. Bake potatoes in a 375°F oven until golden brown, 10 to 20 minutes. Check about halfway through baking time to be sure potatoes brown evenly; give baking sheet a clockwise turn if needed. Carefully transfer baked chips onto paper towels to drain.

3. *Mix crème fraîche:* While potatoes are baking, mix crème fraîche and chives in a small bowl; set aside.

4. *Cook scallops:* Cut each scallop crosswise into 4 slices. Place slices in a single layer on a baking sheet lined with parchment paper. Bake in a 375°F oven until scallops are just opaque at edges and moist in the center, 1 to 2 minutes.

5. *Serve:* For each serving, place a potato chip at the center of plate. Top with a slice of scallop, a spoonful of caviar, and a little of the crème fraîche mixture. Repeat layering, using 3 more potato chips, 3 scallop slices, and remaining caviar and crème fraîche. Garnish each serving with frisée.

The game is up

One of the most celebrated offerings at Patina is the Wild Game Menu. Every autumn, Chef Joachim Splichal offers a series of dishes that highlight the uniquely pungent flavors and textures that can only come from the wild. Some of the game that has been served over the years includes venison, hare, grouse, partridge, wild pigeon, pheasant, woodcock, and wild boar.

A quick perusal of last fall's menu revealed that no bear was being offered. If Chef Splichal is interested, the Peter Michael crew can tell him where to get one.

CHARLIE TROTTER

his own restaurant in Chicago, he embarked on a tour of the world's finest dining

establishments. He was looking for a standard of excellence in food, wine, service,

and ambience, not on which to base his restaurant, but to provide a benchmark of

expectations that he would continuously try to exceed.

To do more, to do it better, ultimately, to do it

as only he can is the driving force behind

Charlie Trotter, and is very much reflected in his

eponymous restaurant. Charlie Trotter's opened in 1987, and is located in a

renovated two-story 1908 townhouse in the Lincoln Park neighborhood of Chicago.

From the beginning, the restaurant won both rave reviews and prestigious awards,

yet it is constantly evolving as Trotter looks for better ways to present what he

describes as a "highly personal cuisine combining impeccable products, French

techniques, and Asian influences."

In truth, the menus are always changing. Trotter, whose father was a jazz musician (among other things), is a firm believer in improvisation and takes pride in never making a recipe the same way twice. "We've received some extraordinary reviews," says Trotter. "But you have to make sure that what you're doing remains lively and vital, and doing the same thing over and over again rarely accomplishes that." No matter how often the dishes change, there will always be the perfect wine to accompany them. The ever-expanding wine cellars house more than 25,000 bottles, and the menu offers more than 1,600 selections. It is, quite simply, one of the best wine collections in the world.

Early on, he made the decision to stop offering dishes à la carte, and went with a set Grand Degustation Menu, a progression of 10 to 12 individual courses, each displaying a different aspect of the chef's prowess. Creations such as diver scallop and black truffle wrapped in caul fat with saffron fettuccine noodles, portobello mushrooms, and rosemary; or olive-oil poached roma tomatoes with English peas, hedgehog mushrooms, and pea and tomato juices are examples of a style that is both delicate and intense, blending boldly contrasting flavors in perfect harmony. A Vegetable Degustation Menu is also offered, as well as Charlie's Spontaneous Menu, which is served to clients seated at the Chef's Table in the middle of the bustling kitchen.

Some things do not change, however. The same staff, including Trotter, works every night the restaurant is open, and the result is service that manages to be both formally precise and warmly congenial. In addition, no cocktails are served, and Trotter rarely uses butter or cream, preferring to sauce with infused oils, vegetable juices, and stock reductions. "I do not want guests walking out of the restaurant feeling as if they overindulged because of excessive cream, butter, or alcohol," says Trotter. "I want them to feel stimulated and alert, knowing that they will be able to look forward to breakfast the following morning. Food doesn't have to be rich to taste good."

Trotter realizes that the combination of complex flavors, cutting-edge ingredients, and his own strong convictions about how the dishes should be experienced means that his restaurant isn't for everyone, particularly in a town that practically invented meat and potatoes. "You have to know what you want to be and what you don't want to be," says Trotter. "That may mean sacrificing a substantial part of a large customer base, but you shouldn't be discouraged if you're certain that you know how to serve those remaining people."

With a legendary restaurant, a highly successful PBS cooking show, a line of cookbooks, and acclaim as one of the world's greatest chefs, it would seem that "those remaining people" Charlie Trotter is serving make up quite a large number indeed.

The 2001 La Carrière has citrus notes of lime and lemon along with a good level of natural acidity, which bring a refreshing sensation to the seasoned white meat in this terrine. The wine's pronounced minerality captures and complements the earthy flavors of the truffles, mascarpone, and black trumpet mushrooms.

The Peter Michael Winery is located on the site of what was once a small town named Kellogg. As a tribute, Pete and Maggie used period photographs of the 19th-century town as inspirations for the winery buildings and offices. The red wine production building is modeled after a barn, the barrel storage rooms after a hotel, and the offices are in a schoolhouse, replete with a bell tower.

The choice of a schoolhouse seems fitting since it was always Pete's goal to educate the American palate about the subtle elegance of French-style wines, while teaching Europeans about the potential of American winemaking.

RABBIT-POLENTA TERRINE WITH TRUFFLED MASCARPONE, BLACK TRUMPET MUSHROOMS, AND CHERVIL

12 Servings

8	rabbit tenderloins (about 12 oz. total)
	Salt and freshly ground pepper
2	tablespoons grapeseed oil
½	cup chopped black truffle
2	large Swiss chard leaves
1½	cups warm cooked polenta
2	tablespoons plus ½ cup olive oil
2	tablespoons chopped fresh chervil
3	cups roasted black trumpet mushrooms (see note)
2	tablespoons sherry wine vinegar
¼	cup white truffle oil
1	cup (8 oz.) mascarpone cheese
½	cup heavy whipping cream
¼	cup loosely packed micro chervil sprouts

Special equipment: Terrine with removable sides (about 2¼ by 8 inches)

1. *Prepare rabbit:* Season rabbit tenderloins with salt and pepper. Heat grapeseed oil in a medium skillet over medium-high heat; add rabbit and cook for 2 minutes on each side. Sprinkle 2 of the rabbit loins with 1 to 2 tablespoons of the chopped truffle, then roll each one up in a chard leaf to enclose snugly; cover and refrigerate remaining cooked rabbit loins. Trim edges of chard leaves even with ends of rabbit loins, if necessary.

2. *Assemble terrine:* Line terrine with plastic wrap, letting edges extend over sides of pan. Mix polenta, the 2 tablespoons olive oil, and the 2 tablespoons chopped chervil; season to taste with salt and pepper. Spoon enough of the polenta mixture into the prepared terrine to fill it a third full. Place the 2 wrapped rabbit loins, end to end, on top of the polenta, cutting them, if necessary, to fit pan. Spoon remaining polenta over the rabbit to fill the pan. Using your fingers, press down firmly to distribute polenta evenly. Fold up plastic wrap to enclose the terrine. Refrigerate until set, about 1 hour.

3. *Make vinaigrette:* Cut the roasted mushrooms into small bite-sized pieces. In a medium-size bowl, combine mushrooms and vinegar. Whisk in truffle oil and remaining ½ cup olive oil. Season to taste with salt and pepper.

4. *Prepare mascarpone cream:* In a medium-size bowl, combine mascarpone and whipping cream. Whip until stiff, then fold in remaining truffle. Season to taste with salt and pepper. Cover and refrigerate until ready to serve, up to 1 hour.

5. *Reheat the terrine:* Unmold the terrine, then tightly wrap again in plastic wrap. With a very sharp knife, cut terrine into 12 slices (each about ¾ inch thick). Remove plastic wrap from each slice. Arrange slices on a baking sheet, then heat in a 350°F oven until warmed through, about 5 minutes.

6. *Serve:* Cut the remaining rabbit loins diagonally into ½-inch slices. For each serving, place a slice of the terrine in center of a plate. Spoon an oval of the mascarpone cream at one corner of the slice. Whisk vinaigrette to blend, then spoon some around the terrine. Place 3 rabbit loin slices around the terrine. Sprinkle with chervil sprouts and freshly ground pepper.

Note: To roast mushrooms, rinse and pat dry 4 cups trimmed black trumpet mushrooms. Combine in a shallow baking pan with 1 clove garlic, 1 small onion (chopped), 1 tablespoon olive oil, ½ cup water, and salt and pepper to taste. Cover and bake in a 325°F oven until tender, 30 to 40 minutes. Cool in the liquid; drain before using.

Schoolhouse in a restaurant

As a product of the Chicago school system, Charlie Trotter found a way to give something back. Twice or three times a week, Chicago area high school students come to his restaurant. There, Chef Trotter and members of his staff give talks on the importance of pursuing excellence regardless of the endeavor. The students are then served one of Trotter's renowned eight-course tasting menus for dinner.

So far, more than 8,000 students have taken part in the "Excellence" program. It's enough to change the way you feel about school meals.

NORMAN VAN AKEN

When asked about the art of being a chef, Norman Van Aken says, "We're interpreters of time and vision through flavors." If this sounds a bit poetic for a cook, perhaps it's because he once aspired to a career writing verse. Those sensibilities were still very much in play when this Florida-based chef founded and named "New World Cuisine." The "New World" harks back to Columbus's landing in the Caribbean, an event that led to a host of new foods, spices, and cooking techniques being introduced to Europe and beyond. The cuisine's native sources include Florida, Cuba, Mexico's

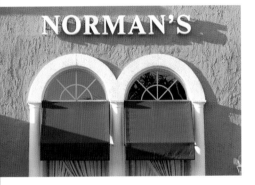

Yucatán Peninsula, the West Indies, Central America, and northern South America. In Van Aken's hands, these sources are fused with European, American, and Asian influences. "My fusion cooking is the result of coupling our native foodstuffs like conch, black beans, mangoes, coconuts, grouper, key limes, and snapper, and the folk-cooking methods intrinsic to the preparation of these goods, with a self-taught type of classical cooking," says the chef. Another important element of the cuisine is the sheer joy and exuberance Van Aken brings to the task. He is a transplanted Midwesterner on a permanent cooking vacation in the tropics, and he and the guests at his Miami restaurant, Norman's, are having the time of their lives.

Norman's is located at 21 Almeria Avenue in the Miami suburb of Coral Gables, just a few blocks south of Miracle Mile. It opened in 1995 in a two-story building with a main dining room featuring two wood-burning ovens and a balcony seating area, but it has since expanded to add a second dining area called the Kitchen–Dining Room. Beautiful tilework, white plastered walls, and dark wooden beams, doorframes, and furniture give the space a hacienda feel, avoiding the pastel fervor that dominates southern Florida. With cooks working the ovens in the main room, an open kitchen in the new space and waiters bustling in between, the theaters of preparation and presentation are inextricably entwined.

Guests have the choice of ordering à la carte or selecting a five-course tasting menu with an optional wine pairing. Both menus change regularly to take advantage of changing ingredients and inspiration, but there are a number of permanent signature dishes such as conch chowder with coconut milk, and peppered venison with ancho pomegranate jam. Appetizers may include pan-cooked Peeky Toe crab cakes with West Indian guacamole, island chips, and salsas; fricassee of Louisiana crawfish and morels with green

asparagus and garlic emulsion; and My Down Island French Toast with Curaçao-scented and seared foie gras, griddled brioche, passion fruit caramel, and gingery candied lime zest. Past entrées include rum and pepper painted grouper on a mango-habanero mojo with a boniato-plantain mash en poblano, and "Mongolian Barbeque" marinated and grilled veal chop with grilled Chinese eggplant and Thai fried rice. Desserts such as key lime pie and the Havana banana split join a substantial cheese selection to round out the meal. The wine list is large, featuring the classic Burgundies, Bordeaux, and California selections, but also eclectic as Van Aken seeks out the ideal pairings for his unique, indigenous ingredients.

Chef Van Aken's original goal was to transform perceptions of South Florida. Though it is well known for its lush landscape, beaches, blend of cultures, and exotic wildlife, he wanted it to be just as renowned for its food. He has achieved that and more. With a series of successful cookbooks and, now, with the opening of a Norman's in Orlando and, most recently, in Los Angeles, Van Aken has spread the word and tantalizing flavors of New World Cuisine to the Gulf Coast and the West Coast as well. What began as an effort to elevate a region has now left that region entirely to stand on its own as a celebrated part of our national taste. "Now it's understood when someone says New World Cuisine," says Van Aken. It just goes to show that, while you might not be able to take the boy out of Florida, you can take his Florida cooking just about anywhere.

The 2001 Belle Côte is an artful pairing for this dish. The wine's richness, power, and natural acidity complement the creamy flesh of the mussels, while its intense bouquet and mild spiciness (white and gray pepper) go hand in hand with the tangy fresh salsa.

The Wappos

Knights Valley was once part of the territory of the Wappo tribe of Native Americans. They viewed Mount St. Helena as a sacred mountain and, for more than 4,000 years, the tribe farmed and hunted in the area while making camp at the nearby geysers and hot springs. Two old Wappo trails, one heading west to the Pacific and the other south to the Napa Valley, intersect near the site of Peter Michael Winery.

The name Wappo is actually an Americanization of the Spanish word guapo, or brave. The tribe earned that name through its fierce resistance to Spanish missionary efforts. Many descendents of the tribe still live in Sonoma County today.

MUSSELS CALLAO (CHILLED MUSSELS WITH SALSA)

6 Servings

3	dozen mussels in shells
1	cup Simple Court Bouillon (page 192) or water
½	cup fresh corn kernels, sautéed in 2 teaspoons extra-virgin olive oil for 30 seconds, then cooled
2	medium tomatoes, peeled, seeded, and chopped
⅓	cup peeled, seeded, and minced cucumber
½	small red onion, minced
1	Scotch Bonnet chili, seeded and minced
2	cloves garlic, minced
2	tablespoons extra-virgin olive oil
1½	tablespoons lemon juice
2	tablespoons chopped cilantro leaves
	Kosher salt and freshly toasted and ground pepper (see note)

1. *Cook mussels:* Just before cooking, remove the beard from each mussel by pulling off with a sharp tug; then scrub mussels with a stiff brush and rinse well. In a deep skillet, bring court bouillon to a boil over high heat. Add mussels; cover and cook until shells open, 2 to 4 minutes. Discard any mussels that do not open. Drain mussels; transfer to a large bowl and refrigerate until cold.

2. *Make salsa:* In a bowl, combine corn, tomatoes, cucumber, onion, chili, and garlic. Stir in oil, lemon juice, and cilantro. Season to taste with salt and pepper. Let stand for about 5 minutes for flavors to blend.

3. *Serve:* Remove and discard the top half of each mussel shell. Detach the meat from the lower shell, leaving meat in the shell. Arrange the mussels on a platter. Spoon a dollop of salsa over each mussel. Serve immediately.

Note: To toast peppercorns, spread in a shallow pan and bake in a 250°F oven for 20 minutes. Let stand until cool before grinding.

The Caribs and the Arawaks

The Caribs and the Arawaks were the indigenous tribes living on the Caribbean islands where Christopher Columbus first made landfall in America. In essence, they were the first users of many of the ingredients of Norman Van Aken's New World Cuisine. They employed pit-style barbecuing and lived on a diet of seafood, small game, yams, cassavas, taro roots, corn, legumes, guavas, pineapples, and chili peppers.

As with so many Native American tribes, the Caribs and the Arawaks were decimated by disease and battles with the European explorers, but Van Aken and other chefs continue to pay homage to their culinary ingenuity and taste.

APPENDIX

BASIC RECIPES

PÂTE SUCRÉE

*Pastry for 8- to 9-inch-square or
10 ½- to 11-inch-round tart pan*

1½   cups all-purpose flour

⅓   cup powdered sugar

½   cup (4 oz.) cold butter, diced

1   large egg yolk

1 to 3 tablespoons cold water

1. In food processor work bowl, combine flour and sugar; whirl to combine. Add butter and whirl, using on/off bursts, until mixture forms particles the size of small peas. With motor running, add egg yolk and whirl just until combined. Add water as needed until pastry begins to cling together.

2. With your hands, press pastry into a flattened ball or square, enclose in plastic wrap, and refrigerate until cold, at least 1 hour. Roll out on a floured surface as directed in tart recipe.

FORTIFIED VENISON STOCK

About 1½ cups stock

---

2   tablespoons butter

2 to 3 pounds venison bones

1   leek

3   carrots, coarsely chopped

2   onions, coarsely chopped

3   stalks celery

2   tablespoons tomato paste

1   bay leaf

5   parsley sprigs

5   whole peppercorns

5   whole coriander seeds

   Chicken stock

1. Melt butter in a large roasting pan in oven as it preheats to 400°F; remove pan from oven and add venison bones, turning to coat with butter. Return pan to oven and roast until bones are browned, about 15 minutes. While bones are browning, thoroughly rinse leek, remove root and coarse outer leaves, then slice about ¼ inch thick. To bones add leek, carrots, onions, and celery; return to oven and bake until vegetables begin to brown, about 15 minutes longer.

2. Transfer vegetables and bones to a large stockpot; add tomato paste, bay leaf, parsley, peppercorns, and coriander. Stir about 1 cup chicken stock into roasting pan, scraping bottom to mix in brown bits; pour over mixture in stockpot. Then add enough more chicken stock to cover mixture by about 1 inch. Bring to a boil over medium-high heat, then reduce heat to low, cover, and simmer for 4 hours. During cooking, occasionally skim off and discard any scum that rises to surface.

3. Strain stock into a bowl, discarding bones, vegetables, and seasonings. Return stock to a smaller pan and cook, uncovered, until reduced to about 1½ cups. Cool, cover, and refrigerate for up to 24 hours; or freeze for longer storage.

FISH FUMET

About 3 cups fumet

1   pound bones and trimmings of any white fish, rinsed to remove any blood

1   medium onion, thinly sliced

      Juice of 1 lemon

½   teaspoon salt

1½   teaspoons white peppercorns

½   cup dry white wine

1   bay leaf

1. In a heavy 3½- to 4-quart pan, combine fish bones and trimmings, onion, lemon juice, salt, peppercorns, wine, and bay leaf. Place over medium-high heat, cover, and let bones steam for 5 to 10 minutes. Then add 3½ cups cold water and bring mixture to a boil. Skim and discard froth that rises to surface. Reduce heat and simmer, uncovered, for 45 minutes.

2. Strain stock through dampened cheesecloth or a very fine sieve into a bowl, discarding bones and seasonings. Cool, cover, and refrigerate for up to 24 hours; or freeze for longer storage.

SIMPLE COURT BOUILLON

About 3½ cups

½   onion, diced

1   large carrot, diced

2   stalks celery, diced

1   small bulb garlic, cut in half horizontally

1   small bulb fennel, trimmed and diced

12   small white mushrooms, rinsed, patted dry, and quartered

1   tablespoon peppercorns, toasted and bruised (see note)

1   tablespoon coriander seeds, toasted (see note)

2   bay leaves, broken in halves

      Zest of 1 lemon, removed in strips with a vegetable peeler

      Zest of 1 orange, removed in strips with a vegetable peeler

2 or 3   sprigs thyme, coarsely chopped

2 or 3   sprigs basil, coarsely chopped

2 or 3   sprigs tarragon, roughly chopped

1   cup dry white wine

6   cups cold water

1. In a small stockpot, combine onion, carrot, celery, garlic, fennel, mushrooms, peppercorns, coriander, bay leaves, lemon and orange zests, thyme, basil, tarragon, wine, and water. Bring almost to a boil over medium-high heat. Reduce heat and simmer gently, uncovered, for 30 minutes.

2. Remove from heat and let stock steep for at least 2 hours to infuse flavors. Then strain through dampened cheesecloth or a very fine sieve into a bowl, discarding solids. Cover and refrigerate for up to 3 days; or freeze for longer storage.

Note: To toast spices, place them in a small skillet over medium heat, toasting until aromatic. Cool, then (to bruise) pound with a mortar and pestle until slightly broken up.

BROWN CHICKEN STOCK

About 3 quarts

10   pounds chicken bones

4   medium carrots (unpeeled),
      sliced 1 inch thick

2   medium yellow onions,
      coarsely chopped

1   cup tomato paste

3½   cups dry white wine

      Water

1. Spread chicken bones in a large roasting pan. Place in a 400°F oven and roast, uncovered, turning once, for 1½ hours. Mix in carrots and onions, then return to oven and continue to roast until bones and vegetables are browned, about 45 minutes longer. Mix in tomato paste, return to oven, and roast for 5 minutes longer.

2. Lift out bones and vegetables and transfer to a large stockpot. Pour off and discard fat from roasting pan. Add about half of the wine to roasting pan, place over medium heat, and scrape up brown bits from pan; add this mixture and remaining wine to stockpot. Add enough water to cover bones by 4 inches. Place over medium-low heat and bring mixture to a simmer.

3. Reduce heat to low, cover, and cook for 10 hours, occasionally skimming and discarding scum that rises to the surface. Add water during cooking, if necessary, to keep bones covered by 2 inches of liquid.

4. Strain stock through a fine sieve into a clean pan, discarding solids. Bring stock to a gentle boil over medium heat and cook, uncovered, until reduced to 3 quarts. Cool, cover, and refrigerate for up to 2 days; or freeze for longer storage.

ADDITIONAL CHEFS' RECIPES

Daniel Boulud

MELON SALAD WITH LEMONGRASS SHRIMP

4 Servings

1½	pounds large shrimp, shelled and deveined
6	tablespoons extra-virgin olive oil
2	teaspoons finely grated peeled ginger
2	teaspoons finely chopped lemongrass
	Finely grated zest of 1 lime
	Juice of 2 limes
1/8	teaspoon Tabasco
	Salt and freshly ground white pepper
1	ripe honeydew melon
1	ripe, small, round, seedless red watermelon
1	tablespoon finely chopped purple basil leaves
1	tablespoon finely chopped cilantro leaves
	Basil and cilantro leaves, for garnish

1. *Cook shrimp:* In a large pan, bring salted water to a boil. Add shrimp and cook just until opaque in center, 3 to 5 minutes (cut to test). Drain and let cool, then slice each shrimp in half lengthwise.

2. *Make dressing:* In a small bowl, combine olive oil, ginger, lemongrass, lime zest and juice, and Tabasco; whisk until blended. Season to taste with salt and pepper; set dressing aside.

3. *Prepare melons:* Cut honeydew in half, scoop out and discard seeds, and cut away and discard rind. Cut watermelon in half and cut away and discard rind. Cut each melon half into ⅛-inch-thick slices. Using a round cutter slightly smaller than the diameter of a champagne coupe or 8- to 12-ounce martini glass, cut 16 honeydew rounds and 16 watermelon rounds.

4. *Assemble salads:* Set out 4 champagne coupes or 8- to 12-ounce martini glasses. Set aside 4 perfect watermelon rounds for top of each salad. For each salad, layer 2 watermelon rounds and 2 honeydew rounds in a glass, sprinkling each layer with a little of the dressing and chopped basil, cilantro, and salt and pepper to taste. Then arrange a fourth of the shrimp halves in concentric circles on top of the melon; season shrimp with dressing, basil, cilantro, and salt and pepper. Then add 2 honeydew rounds and 2 watermelon rounds, seasoning each layer as before and ending with a perfect watermelon slice on top. Sprinkle salads with any remaining dressing. Cover lightly and refrigerate until well chilled, at least 1 hour.

5. *Serve:* Garnish each salad with a basil leaf and a cilantro leaf.

John Campbell

SALAD OF SUMMER VEGETABLES

4 Servings

Smoked Oil Vinaigrette

3   tablespoons smoked oil (see note)

1   tablespoon white wine vinegar

       Salt and freshly ground pepper

Truffle Mayonnaise

½   cup homemade mayonnaise (made without vinegar)

2   teaspoons truffle oil

¾   teaspoon truffle vinegar or white wine vinegar

1   teaspoon grated truffle

Vegetables

1   large artichoke

       Lemon juice

8   medium-size (1½- to 2-in.-diameter) smooth-skinned potatoes

1   small celery root (about 1 lb.), peeled and cut into ¼-inch cubes

3   cups cauliflower florets (12 to 14 oz.), thinly sliced vertically

3   tablespoons corn oil

⅓   cup butter

1   ounce small wild mushrooms, such as chanterelles, rinsed and patted dry

About 2 cups assorted baby lettuce leaves and fresh herbs (such as parsley, chervil, and chives), rinsed, drained, and chilled

1. *Make Smoked Oil Vinaigrette:* In a small bowl, combine smoked oil, vinegar, and salt and pepper to taste. Whisk until blended; set dressing aside.

2. *Make Truffle Mayonnaise:* In another bowl, combine mayonnaise, truffle oil, vinegar, and truffle; mix well. Cover and refrigerate for up to 24 hours to allow truffle flavor to be absorbed.

3. *Cook artichoke:* Slice off and discard artichoke stem; remove and discard coarse outer leaves, then cut off top third of artichoke; rinse well. Place artichoke in a large pan of boiling, salted water to which lemon juice has been added to prevent darkening. Cover and boil until stem end is tender when pierced, 40 to 45 minutes. Drain and let stand until cool enough to handle. Pull off leaves; scoop out and discard fuzzy choke. Cut artichoke bottom into bite-size cubes; set aside. Reserve leaves for other uses.

4. *Cook potatoes:* In a 3- to 4-quart pan, bring salted water to a boil. Scrub potatoes and add to boiling water; boil gently, partially covered, until potatoes are just tender when pierced, about 20 minutes. Drain well, then let stand until cool enough to handle. Slice unpeeled potatoes about ½ inch thick; set aside.

5. *Cook celery root and cauliflower:* Bring salted water to a boil in a 2- to 3-quart pan; add celery root and cauliflower and boil gently until just tender when pierced, about 5 minutes. Drain, transfer to a bowl of cold water to cool, and drain again; pat dry with paper towels, then set aside.

6. *Sauté vegetables:* In a wide skillet over medium heat, heat about 2 tablespoons of the corn oil. Add potatoes in a single layer and cook, turning carefully, until lightly browned; add butter and continue cooking until butter is foamy. Season potatoes with salt and pepper to taste, then lift out with a spatula and drain on paper towels. To same pan add artichoke, celery root, cauliflower, and mushrooms. Cook until golden brown, adding more oil if needed. Lift out vegetables and drain on paper towels.

7. *Dress greens:* In a bowl, lightly mix baby lettuce and herbs with about a third of the vinaigrette. Reserve remaining vinaigrette for other uses.

8. *Serve:* Thin mayonnaise, if necessary, with a little water to make a pourable consistency. For each salad serving, arrange a fourth of the potatoes in a circle in center of large plate. Top each with a fourth of the artichoke mixture, then a fourth of the greens and herbs. Spoon mayonnaise generously around the potatoes.

Note: To make smoked oil, at least 24 hours before preparing salad, place about 2 cups oak chips in a wide, heavy pan. Place over medium heat, shaking pan occasionally, until chips begin to smoke. Pour ¾ cup vegetable oil into a heatproof bowl. Place bowl in center of chips. Soak a kitchen towel in cold water, wring out, and drape over pan to enclose contents (do not let towel touch hot surface unit). Reduce heat to low and let oil smoke for 30 minutes. Remove bowl with oil and let oil cool to room temperature. Transfer to a covered jar and store in a dark, cool place for up to 3 weeks; or freeze for longer storage. Use remaining oil to add smoke flavor when cooking steak or chicken.

Tom Colicchio

SPICED ROASTED LOBSTER WITH PEA RAVIOLI

4 to 6 servings

Ravioli

12	ounces Fresh Pasta (recipe follows)
2½	cups shelled fresh peas (from 2 to 3 lb. peas in pods)
1	tablespoon peanut oil
1	shallot, minced
½	cup whipping cream
	Kosher salt and freshly ground pepper
	Cornmeal

Sauce

1½	cups Lobster Stock (recipe follows)
1	teaspoon Lobster Spice (recipe follows)
	Peel of ½ orange, cut into thin strips
	Small piece fresh ginger, peeled and smashed
4	cardamom pods
3	tablespoons crème fraîche
2	tablespoons Lobster Butter (recipe follows), cut into several pieces
	Kosher salt
2	teaspoons red peppercorns

Lobster

4	live lobsters (about 1¼ lb. each)
1	tablespoon extra-virgin olive oil
	Kosher salt and freshly ground black pepper
5	tablespoons unsalted butter
2	bay leaves
1	tablespoon chopped fresh chervil or tarragon
1	tablespoon chopped fresh chives
½	cup loosely packed pea shoots

1. *Make pasta:* Using recipe on page 198, prepare pasta and refrigerate as directed.

2. *Make lobster spice:* Using recipe on page 198, make lobster spice.

3. *Make lobster stock:* Remove lobster tail and claws, reserving bodies. Then proceed as directed in recipe on page 198.

4. *Make lobster butter:* Using recipe on page 198, make lobster butter

5. *Make ravioli:* In a large pan over high heat, bring salted water to a boil. Add peas and cook until tender, 3 to 5 minutes. Drain well, rinse with cold water, rinse again, and set aside. Heat oil in a medium-size pan over moderate heat; add shallot and cook, stirring occasionally, until it begins to soften, about 5 minutes. Add 1½ cups of the peas and cook until soft and bright green, 2 to 3 minutes. Add cream and salt and pepper to taste. Simmer, stirring occasionally, for 5 minutes. Cool slightly, then transfer mixture to a blender or food processor. Whirl until puréed. Press purée through a strainer into a bowl.

Lay a sheet of the rolled pasta dough on a work surface. Using half the pea mixture, place spoonfuls in 2 rows of 3 over half the pasta sheet, allowing about 2 inches between spoonfuls. Brush the other half of the sheet lightly with water, then fold it over the first. Press your fingers around each pocket of filling to seal, then cut the ravioli into squares or rounds. Transfer ravioli to a baking sheet dusted with cornmeal. Repeat with remaining dough and filling. Let ravioli dry for about 15 minutes; turn them over and let dry for 15 minutes longer.

6. *Prepare sauce:* In a medium pan, combine lobster stock, lobster spice, orange peel, ginger, and cardamom pods. Bring to a boil, then reduce heat and simmer, uncovered, until reduced to about ½ cup. Remove pan from heat and let stock steep for about 10 minutes. Strain through a fine sieve into a bowl, discarding solids. Wipe out the pan, pour in the strained stock, and place over medium heat until stock simmers gently. Whisk in the crème fraîche and let mixture simmer for a minute, then reduce heat to low. Whisk in lobster butter, one piece at a time. Season to taste with salt. Keep sauce warm over lowest heat, stirring occasionally.

7. *Parboil lobsters:* In a very large pan over high heat, bring salted water to a boil. Wrap lobster tails in a double thickness of plastic wrap. Lower tails into water, weighting them with a heavy plate so they remain submerged; cover and cook for 4 minutes. Rinse well with cold water, drain, and set aside. Then cook lobster claws for 7 minutes, rinse, and drain. Crack claws and tails; remove the meat in large, intact pieces. Carefully lift out tail veins and discard them. Set cooked lobster aside.

8. *Cook ravioli:* Bring salted water to a boil over high heat. Add ravioli and cook until tender, about 3 minutes. Drain ravioli, reserving ¼ cup of the cooking water.

9. *Finish cooking lobster:* In a large skillet over medium-high heat, heat olive oil until it shimmers. Season lobster meat with salt and pepper to taste, then with lobster spice. Add to skillet and cook for 30 seconds; add 2 tablespoons of the butter. Turn the lobster pieces and cook for 30 seconds longer, then reduce heat to low. Add 2 tablespoons of the remaining butter and the bay leaves. Cook, turning lobster in the butter until meat is just firm, about 3 minutes.

10. *Serve:* Arrange lobster in wide serving bowls, dividing it evenly. Wipe out the skillet and melt the remaining 1 tablespoon butter with a little of the reserved pasta cooking water over medium-low heat. Add ravioli, the reserved 1 cup peas, and half of the chervil and chives. Cook until ravioli is heated through. Meanwhile, with a hand mixer or blender, mix sauce until frothy; mix in red peppercorns. Spoon sauce around the lobster. Divide ravioli and peas among bowls. Garnish with remaining chervil, chives, and pea shoots.

Fresh Pasta
12 ounces

2	large eggs, lightly beaten
1	tablespoon extra-virgin olive oil
1 to 2	tablespoons water
2	cups all-purpose flour
	Salt

1. In a small bowl, combine eggs, oil, and water; mix well. In a large bowl, mix flour and a pinch of salt. Make a well in the center of the flour mixture and pour in egg mixture. Using your fingers, gradually work flour into egg mixture until dough holds together. Turn out onto a lightly floured surface and knead until dough is smooth and elastic. Enclose in plastic wrap and refrigerate for at least 1 hour or up to 2 days.

2. Divide the pasta in half. In a pasta machine, roll out half the pasta at a time, starting with widest setting and rolling pasta through each setting twice until you reach the second narrowest setting.

Lobster Spice

½	teaspoon mustard seeds
½	teaspoon coriander seeds
½	teaspoon fennel seeds
1	bay leaf, crumbled
	Cayenne pepper

1. In a small skillet over medium-low heat, combine mustard, coriander, and fennel seeds. Toast until fragrant, 8 to 10 minutes. Transfer spice mixture to a spice grinder or mortar. Add bay leaf and pinch of cayenne; grind or crush with a pestle. If made ahead, cover airtight until ready to use.

Lobster Stock
About 3 cups

4	lobster bodies, split lengthwise
2	tablespoons extra-virgin olive oil
1	onion, chopped
1	leek (white part only), well rinsed and chopped
1	carrot, chopped
1	stalk celery, chopped
1	sprig fresh thyme
	About 6 cups water

1. Remove head sac, tomalley (yellow-colored liver), and any coral-colored roe from body cavities. Discard sac and tomalley; reserve roe for Lobster Butter. Break or cut each body into 4 to 6 pieces.

2. In a large deep pan over medium-low heat, heat the oil. Add onion, leek, carrot, and celery; cook, stirring occasionally, until vegetables are tender, about 20 minutes. Add lobster bodies and thyme, then cook, stirring often, until lobster shells begin to turn red, about 5 minutes. Add water to cover. Bring to a gentle boil and cook, skimming as needed, until stock is flavorful, about 1 hour. Ladle stock through a fine sieve into a deep bowl, discarding solids. If made ahead, cover and refrigerate for up to 1 week or freeze for up to 6 months.

Lobster Butter

	Roe from 1 or 2 lobsters
½	cup (4 oz.) unsalted butter, at room temperature
	Kosher salt

In food processor or blender, combine roe, butter, and a pinch of salt; whirl until mixture is smooth. Scrape butter mixture onto a 5-inch square of plastic wrap. Form into a cylinder-shaped roll in the plastic wrap. Refrigerate until firm, up to 2 days; or freeze for up to 1 month.

Gary Danko

PANCETTA-WRAPPED FROG'S LEGS WITH SUNCHOKE-GARLIC PURÉE, LENTILS, POTATOES, AND PARSLEY SAUCE

6 Servings

Beluga Lentils with Potatoes and Mustard Butter

2	cups beluga lentils, rinsed and sorted to remove debris
½	cup finely chopped onion
3	slices bacon
1	tablespoon kosher salt
1	cup finely diced peeled potato
½	cup (4 oz.) unsalted butter
3	tablespoons minced shallots
1	tablespoon Dijon mustard

Sunchoke-Garlic Purée

2	pounds medium-size sunchokes (also known as Jerusalem artichokes), peeled and cut into 1-inch cubes
2	bulbs garlic, separated into cloves and peeled
	Pinch freshly ground nutmeg
1	sprig thyme
1	bay leaf
	Salt
	Whipping cream

Marinade

2	tablespoons dry red wine, such as Cabernet Sauvignon
1½	teaspoons minced garlic
½	teaspoon kosher salt
1	tablespoon Dijon mustard
¾	teaspoon dried thyme
¾	teaspoon ground coriander
2	tablespoons extra-virgin olive oil

Frog's Legs

18	dressed frog's legs
18	thin slices pancetta
	About 2 tablespoons extra-virgin olive oil
	Kosher salt and freshly ground pepper
½	teaspoon minced fresh dill
½	teaspoon thinly sliced chives

Parsley Sauce

1	tablespoon minced shallot
½	cup dry white wine
½	cup Fish Fumet (page 192)
½	cup bottled clam juice
1	bay leaf
1	sprig thyme
¼	cup whipping cream
6	tablespoons (3 oz.) unsalted butter, cut into chunks
	Salt
6	cloves garlic
¼	cup minced parsley
	Zest of 2 lemons, minced

1. *Prepare lentils and potatoes:* In a medium-size pan, combine lentils, onion, 2 slices of the bacon, and salt; add water to cover by about 1 inch. Bring to a boil, then reduce heat to moderate and cook until lentils are tender, 20 to 30 minutes. Meanwhile, combine potato and remaining bacon slice in another pan; add water to cover by 1 inch. Bring to a boil, then reduce heat slightly and cook just until tender, 10 to 15 minutes. Drain potatoes, discarding bacon; set aside. Drain lentils, discarding bacon and reserving about ½ cup of the cooking liquid. Combine cooked lentils and potatoes in a shallow pan lined with parchment paper.

2. *Make mustard butter:* Melt 1 tablespoon of the butter in a small skillet over medium heat, then sauté shallots until translucent; set aside to cool slightly. In a food processor, combine the remaining 7 tablespoons butter, mustard, and shallots. Whirl to combine well, then transfer mixture to a bowl and set aside.

3. *Make sunchoke purée:* In a 4- to 5-quart pan, combine sunchokes, garlic, nutmeg, thyme, bay leaf, and salt to taste; add water to cover by about 1 inch. Bring to a boil, then reduce heat and simmer until sunchokes are tender when pierced, about 20 minutes. Drain well, then place hot sunchoke mixture in food processor; whirl until smooth, adding cream as needed to make a medium-thick purée. Press through a medium sieve into a bowl. Season to taste with salt.

4. *Prepare marinade:* In a small bowl, combine wine, garlic, salt, mustard, thyme, coriander, and olive oil; mix well.

5. *Prepare frog's legs:* With the back of a knife, scrape meat from narrower end of each leg toward meatier end to resemble a chicken drummette. Place prepared frog's legs in a wide plastic container, add marinade, and mix lightly to coat well. Let stand for about 10 minutes. Then wrap each leg in a slice of pancetta; cover and refrigerate while preparing sauce.

6. *Make parsley sauce:* In a heavy 1½-to 2-quart stainless steel pan, combine shallot, wine, fumet, clam juice, bay leaf, and thyme. Bring to a boil, then boil over medium-high heat until reduced to about a third of original volume. Add cream and boil until mixture is foamy. Whisk in butter, a chunk at a time. Season to taste with salt. Pour through a fine strainer into a bowl, pressing down on solids; discard solids. Keep warm over hot but not boiling water. In a small pan of boiling water, blanch garlic for about 30 seconds; drain well and mince fine. In another bowl, combine minced garlic, parsley, and lemon zest; set mixture aside.

7. *Cook frog's legs:* Heat olive oil in a sauté pan over medium-high heat. Add frog's legs, about 3 at a time, and sear until browned on both sides. As frog's legs are browned, transfer to a shallow pan in a single layer and place in a 350°F oven for 2 to 5 minutes.

8. *Serve:* While frog's legs are cooking, reheat lentils and potatoes in a sauté pan, adding mustard butter to taste. Add parsley-garlic mixture to warm sauce. Reheat sunchoke purée. For each serving, spoon sunchoke purée and lentils into a wide, shallow soup bowl; arrange 3 frog's legs around lentils. Spoon warm sauce around the frog's legs. Garnish with minced dill and sliced chives.

Ken Frank

CHOCOLATE ESPRESSO SOUFFLÉ

4 Servings

5	ounces bittersweet chocolate, coarsely chopped
	Unsalted butter, for soufflé dishes
	Granulated sugar, for soufflé dishes
4	large egg whites
1	tablespoon powdered sugar, plus additional sugar for garnish
3	large egg yolks
3½	tablespoons freshly brewed espresso coffee
	Whipped cream or espresso ice cream (optional)

Special equipment: Four individual soufflé dishes, each about 3 inches in diameter and about 1½ inches deep

1. In the top of a double boiler, melt chocolate over barely simmering water until chocolate is just warm to the touch.

2. Prepare soufflé dishes: Generously butter insides of the dishes, then thoroughly coat with granulated sugar (for each, pour in about 2 tablespoons sugar, rotating to coat evenly; pour out remaining sugar). Set soufflé dishes aside.

3. Whisk egg whites until frothy, then beat in 1 tablespoon powdered sugar. Whisk until firm, smooth peaks form (do not overbeat). Set egg whites aside.

4. Transfer warm chocolate to a large bowl and whisk in egg yolks. Then quickly mix in espresso until mixture is smooth. With a rubber spatula, gently but thoroughly fold in beaten egg whites. Fill each of the prepared soufflé dishes to the top with the soufflé mixture.

5. Bake in a 400°F oven for 8 minutes. Quickly sprinkle soufflés with powdered sugar and serve immediately, garnishing, if desired, with whipped cream or ice cream.

Suzanne Goin

LAMB TAGINE WITH COUSCOUS, SAFFRON ONIONS, AND CUMIN YOGURT

6 Servings

Lamb Shanks

6	lamb shanks, 10 to 12 ounces each
1	red onion, sliced
4	cloves garlic, smashed
½	bunch cilantro, roughly chopped
2	tablespoons olive oil
1	tablespoon salt
1	teaspoon freshly ground pepper
	Cilantro sprigs

Spice Mixture

1	chile d'arbol, ground
6	tablespoons cumin seeds, toasted and ground (see note)
6	tablespoons fennel seeds, toasted and ground
3	tablespoons coriander seeds, toasted and ground
1	tablespoon paprika
1	teaspoon cayenne pepper

Saffron Onions

1	tablespoon unsalted butter
3	medium onions, thinly sliced
¼	teaspoon saffron threads, toasted and pounded (see note)
	Salt and freshly ground pepper

Braised Vegetables

1	bulb fennel, trimmed and cut into thin wedges
1	large onion, thinly sliced
6	canned tomatoes with ½ cup of their juices
1	cup dry white wine
2	cups lamb stock or veal stock

Couscous

2	cups couscous
2	tablespoons extra-virgin olive oil
1	small onion, finely diced
	Pinch saffron threads
¼	teaspoon cayenne pepper
1	teaspoon ground cinnamon
¼	teaspoon freshly ground pepper
1	teaspoon salt
2	cups chicken stock, vegetable stock, or water

Cumin Yogurt

1	cup whole milk yogurt
¼	teaspoon kosher salt
	Pinch freshly ground pepper
½	teaspoon ground toasted cumin seeds (see note)

1. *Marinate lamb shanks:* Place lamb shanks in a large bowl. Add red onion, garlic, chopped cilantro, and 1 tablespoon of the olive oil. Cover and refrigerate for at least 8 hours or up to a day.

2. *Prepare spice mixture:* In a small bowl, combine ground chile, cumin, fennel, and coriander seeds, paprika, and cayenne. Set aside.

3. *Season marinated lamb:* Remove lamb from refrigerator and add salt, pepper, and ¼ cup of the spice mixture. Let stand at room temperature for 1 hour.

4. *Prepare Saffron Onions:* Melt butter in wide, heavy skillet over low heat. Add onions and saffron, then season to taste with salt and pepper. Cook, stirring occasionally, until onions are very soft but not brown, about 15 minutes. Transfer onions to a wide, deep braising pan; set aside.

5. *Sear lamb and braise vegetables:* To the same pan in which onions were cooked, add the remaining 1 tablespoon olive oil; place pan over high heat. Brown lamb shanks, 2 or 3 at a time, on all sides; reserve garlic and onions from marinade. As lamb shanks are well browned, add to pan with saffron onions. To pan in which lamb was browned, add fennel and onion along with garlic and onion from the marinade. Reduce heat to medium and cook, stirring often, until vegetables begin to caramelize. Stir in tomatoes and their juices, using a wooden spoon to scrape up brown bits from pan. Add wine, increase heat to medium-high, and cook until reduced by about half. Add lamb stock and bring mixture to a boil. Pour liquid with vegetables over lamb shanks.

6. *Bake lamb shanks:* Cover pan tightly with plastic wrap, then with heavy aluminum foil. Place in a 325°F oven and bake until lamb is very tender when pierced, 2½ to 3 hours. Uncover and continue to bake until lamb browns slightly, about 15 minutes. Lift lamb shanks from braising liquid, place in a shallow pan, and set aside. Let liquid cool, then skim and discard surface fat.

7. *Make couscous:* Place couscous in a bowl. Heat oil in a 2-quart pan over medium heat; add onion and cook, stirring occasionally, until translucent, 3 to 5 minutes. Stir in saffron, cayenne, cinnamon, pepper, and salt; cook for about 1 minute. Add chicken stock and bring mixture to a boil; pour over couscous, stirring to mix in onions and seasonings. Cover with plastic wrap and let stand for 15 to 20 minutes.

8. *Prepare Cumin Yogurt:* In a bowl, combine yogurt, salt, pepper, and cumin; set aside.

9. *Serve:* Return lamb to 325˚ F oven until heated through and well browned. Reheat skimmed liquid and vegetables, then spoon over lamb; garnish with cilantro sprigs. Serve with coucous and yogurt.

Note: To toast spices, place in a small pan over medium heat until fragrant, 4 to 5 minutes.

J. Joho

MICHIGAN CHERRY PISTACHIO GRATIN SOUFFLÉ

4 Servings

Cherries

1	cup dry red wine, such as Cabernet Sauvignon
¼	cup red port
¼	cup granulated sugar
1	cinnamon stick (about 3 inches long)
1	pound Michigan sweet cherries, stemmed and pitted
1	tablespoon cornstarch

Soufflé

	Butter and granulated sugar for soufflé dishes
⅓	cup plus 2 tablespoons granulated sugar
2	tablespoons all-purpose flour
2	teaspoons cornstarch
¾	cup milk
2	large egg yolks
1	teaspoon butter
1½	tablespoons pistachio paste (see note)
5	large egg whites
	Powdered sugar

Special equipment: 4 individual soufflé dishes or ramekins, each about 4½ inches in diameter and about 1½ inches deep.

1. *Prepare cherries:* In a 1½-to 2-quart nonreactive pan, combine red wine, port, and granulated sugar. Place over medium-high heat, stirring until sugar is dissolved.

Add cinnamon stick, reduce heat, and simmer for 10 minutes. Add cherries and cook for 5 minutes longer. Then add cornstarch, stirring until thickened and clear, about 1 minute. Remove from heat, discard cinnamon stick, and set cherries aside until cool.

2. *Prepare soufflé dishes:* Generously butter 4 individual 4½-inch soufflé dishes (each about 1¼-cup capacity). Sprinkle with sugar, tipping and shaking to coat evenly. Drain cherries and divide equally into the dishes. Preheat oven to 375°F.

3. *Make soufflé mixture:* In a heavy, non-reactive 1- to 1½-quart pan, combine the ⅓ cup granulated sugar, flour, and cornstarch; mix well. Whisk in milk, then egg yolks. Cook, stirring constantly, over medium heat until mixture thickens, 3 to 5 minutes. Remove from heat and whisk in butter and pistachio paste; transfer mixture to a large bowl and set aside. In a large bowl, beat egg whites at high speed until foamy; then beat in remaining 2 tablespoons granulated sugar, continuing to beat until egg whites form stiff, distinct peaks. Fold about half the egg whites thoroughly into the egg yolk mixture. Then gently fold in remaining egg whites. Divide into prepared soufflé dishes.

4. *Bake and serve soufflés:* Bake until puffy and golden brown, 15 to 20 minutes. Quickly sift powdered sugar over each soufflé, then serve immediately.

Note: Pistachio paste, imported from Italy, is available in bakers' supply stores; almond paste can be substituted, if desired.

Thomas Keller

GRILLED SNAKE RIVER RANCH "CALOTTE DE BOEUF"

With Stuffed Cipollini, Upside-Down Yellow Corn Cake, and Truffle "Velouté" — 6 Servings

---

Stuffed Cipollini

12	cipollini (small flat onions)
	Vegetable oil
4¼	cups hot chicken stock
2	sprigs thyme
¾	cup finely diced bacon
2½	teaspoons finely diced black truffle
¾	cup bone marrow, diced
1	heaping teaspoon chopped chives
1	heaping teaspoon chopped flat-leaf parsley
⅓	cup fine crumbs of crustless brioche
	Salt and freshly ground pepper

Upside-Down Yellow Corn Cakes

½	cup (4 oz.) unsalted butter
	Vegetable oil cooking spray
⅔	cup fresh corn kernels
¾	cup yellow cornmeal
⅓	cup sugar
5	tablespoons all-purpose flour
	Salt and freshly ground pepper
6	large egg whites

Truffle "Velouté"

2½	tablespoons bone marrow (see note)
2	tablespoons all-purpose flour
¾	cup truffle juice
½	cup whipping cream
2½	tablespoons milk
1	teaspoon truffle vinegar
	Salt and freshly ground pepper
	Chervil sprigs, chopped truffles, and chives

Grilled Beef

6	tender, boneless beef steaks (3 oz. each), trimmed of fat
	Kosher salt
	Freshly ground pepper
	Vegetable oil

Special equipment: Parchment paper; six ¼-cup aluminum baking cups

1. *Cook cipollini:* Peel cipollini, leaving root ends intact. To a heavy, straight-sided ovenproof pan wide enough to hold all the cipollini in a single layer, add enough oil to make a film in pan bottom. Place over medium heat, add cipollini, and cook until lightly browned on all sides. Pour in stock, add thyme, and bring to a simmer. Cut a round of parchment paper the same size as pan; place over cipollini, then transfer pan to a 350°F oven and bake until they are tender when pierced, about 30 minutes. Lift cipollini from liquid; set aside. Strain cooking liquid through a fine sieve, reserving liquid.

2. *Make stuffing for cipollini:* Cook bacon in a skillet over medium heat until crisp; lift out bacon and drain on paper towels. Pour bacon fat into a bowl and set aside. Pour cooking liquid into a pan, then boil over medium-high heat until reduced to a saucelike consistency; set aside. In a bowl, combine bacon, truffle, marrow, a fourth of the bacon fat, reduced cooking liquid, chives, parsley, and brioche crumbs. Season to taste with salt and pepper. Cover and refrigerate while preparing onions.

3. *Trim and stuff onions:* Trim and discard outer layer and root from each onion, being careful to keep onion intact. With tip of a small knife or scissors, make a cavity in each onion. Spoon stuffing into onions, using as much as possible (freeze any remaining stuffing for other uses). Brush onions with reserved bacon fat and place in a shallow baking pan; sprinkle with remaining brioche crumbs. If made ahead, cover and refrigerate for up to 24 hours.

4. *Make brown butter for corn cakes:* In a small pan over low heat, melt until butter it is amber colored. As butter heats, skim off and discard crust that rises to top. When butter is amber colored, strain butter through a very fine wire strainer; set aside.

5. *Prepare and bake corn cakes:* Coat six ¼-cup aluminum baking cups with cooking spray. Divide corn into prepared baking cups; set aside. For batter, in a bowl whisk together cornmeal, sugar, flour, and salt and pepper to taste. With a whisk, blend in the egg whites until smooth. Add 5 to 6 tablespoons of the brown butter to make a thick batter. Spoon batter over corn in baking cups, filling each about three-fourths full. Bake in a 325°F oven until cakes are puffed and golden brown, 10 to 12 minutes. Let cool on a rack for 10 minutes, then carefully invert out of baking cups into a shallow baking pan; if necessary, trim tops so cakes sit flat. Set aside until ready to serve.

6. *Make truffle velouté:* In a heavy 1½-quart pan, melt bone marrow over medium heat. Whisk in the flour and cook, stirring constantly, for 2 to 3 minutes. Remove from heat and gradually stir in truffle juice. Return to heat and cook, stirring constantly until smooth. Stir in cream and milk; cook, stirring, until thickened and smooth. Whisk in vinegar, then reduce heat to very low and cook for 20 minutes. Strain through a fine sieve; season to taste with salt and pepper. Set aside until ready to serve.

7. *Cook beef and serve:* In a 350°F oven, reheat stuffed cipollini and corn cakes. Season steaks with salt and pepper to taste; coat lightly with oil. Cook on a preheated grill over medium-high heat, turning once, until well browned, 8 to 10 minutes total for medium-rare. Meanwhile, warm velouté in a small pan over medium-low heat. Lift steaks from grill and let rest for about 4 minutes. On each plate arrange 2 cipollini and 1 corn cake. Slice beef thin and arrange slices over corn cake. Spoon velouté around each plate. Garnish with chervil sprigs, chopped truffles, and chives.

Note: If bone marrow is not available, you may substitute beef fat or butter.

Patrick O'Connell

PINEAPPLE SKILLET TARTS

10 to 12 Servings

Coconut Ice Cream

4	cups whole milk
2	cups whipping cream
1	cup sugar
7	large egg yolks
3¾	cups canned coconut milk (stir before measuring), such as Coco Lopez

Coconut Shells

2	cups chopped semisweet chocolate
1	cup finely chopped macadamia nuts

Crêpes

2	cups all-purpose flour
6	tablespoons (3 oz.) unsalted butter, melted and cooled
¼	cup sugar
3	large eggs
	Salt

About 1 cup whole milk

Skillet Tarts

2	large ripe pineapples, peeled, cored, and cut lengthwise into quarters
6	tablespoons (3 oz.) cold unsalted butter, cut into bits, plus 3 tablespoons unsalted butter for pan
¾	cup toasted, coarsely ground macadamia nuts
½	cup sugar
¾	cup whipping cream
	Vegetable oil cooking spray
½	cup 151-proof rum

Special equipment: 2 ½-quart (or larger) ice cream maker, parchment paper, 8 small balloons, 7-inch nonstick skillet or seasoned crêpe pan

1. *Make ice cream:* In a heavy 4-quart pan over medium heat, combine milk, cream, and sugar. Bring to a boil, stirring to dissolve sugar; remove from heat. In top of a double boiler or a large stainless steel bowl, combine egg yolks and coconut milk. Slowly whisk in hot cream mixture. Place over simmering water and cook, stirring with a whisk, until mixture thickens enough to coat the back of a metal spoon. Remove from heat and strain through a fine sieve into a bowl. Cool, then refrigerate until cold. Freeze in an ice cream maker according to manufacturer's directions.

2. *Prepare coconut shells:* Line a large baking sheet with parchment paper. Blow up balloons to about 3-inch diameter. Place chocolate in a metal bowl over hot but not boiling water until melted; remove from heat. Spread nuts in a shallow pan. For each shell, dip an inflated balloon halfway into the melted chocolate to coat well, then dip into nuts to add a nut coating. Place dipped balloon on the prepared baking sheet, then repeat with remaining balloons. Place baking sheet with balloons in freezer until chocolate is hard, about 30 minutes. Remove balloons from freezer, pop them with knife tip, and remove from chocolate shells. Carefully fill each shell with coconut ice cream, smoothing top with a small spatula. Return filled shells to freezer. Cover lightly and keep in freezer until ready to serve (up to 3 days).

3. *Make crêpe batter:* In a food processor or blender, combine flour, melted butter, sugar, eggs, a pinch of salt, and ¾ cup of the milk; whirl until smooth. Add more milk, if necessary, to make a pourable batter; whirl again. Cover and refrigerate for at least 1 hour or up to 1 day.

4. *Prepare skillet tarts:* Line 2 large baking sheets with parchment paper; set aside. Cut pineapple quarters crosswise into ⅛-inch-thick slices. For each skillet tart, melt ¼ teaspoon of the butter in 7-inch nonstick skillet or seasoned crêpe pan over medium heat. Remove from heat and ladle in 3 tablespoons of the crêpe batter, tipping and tilting pan to coat evenly. Sprinkle the crêpe with 1 tablespoon of the nuts. Return pan to medium heat until crêpe begins to set but looks moist on surface. Remove pan from heat and quickly overlap pineapple slices in concentric circles to cover surface of crêpe. Return pan to heat and sprinkle pineapple with 2 teaspoons sugar and a few bits of cold butter. Lift edge of crêpe to check for browning. When golden brown, loosen the crêpe with a flexible heatproof spatula and carefully flip crêpe over in pan. Continue to cook until sugar on underside begins to caramelize. Drizzle 1 tablespoon of the cream around the edge; tip and tilt pan so cream flows under the crêpe and blends with the sugar.

5. *Unmold skillet tarts:* Have ready a round flat-bottomed pan, such as a layer cake pan. Invert pan and coat bottom with cooking spray. Place pan over skillet and invert skillet tart out onto pan, then slide tart onto prepared baking sheet. Repeat process to make remaining skillet tarts to make 10 to 12 in all.

6. *Serve:* Slide a skillet tart onto each plate. Using a melon ball cutter, scoop out a hollow in center of ice cream in each coconut shell (return remaining ice cream to freezer for another use). Place a coconut shell in center or alongside skillet tart. In a small, long-handled metal pan, heat rum until barely warm to the touch. Ignite and carefully ladle a spoonful of the flaming rum into hollow in each coconut shell, then serve flaming.

Michel Richard

VEAL BLANQUETTE

6 Servings

4	pounds breast of veal (cut into several pieces) or veal shanks
1	clove
1	onion
2	carrots, sliced
1	stalk celery
6	parsley sprigs
1	sprig thyme
	Salt and freshly ground pepper
1	tablespoon butter
1	tablespoon vegetable oil
1	pound pearl onions, peeled
1	pound small white mushrooms, rinsed and patted dry
½	cup crème fraîche
	Juice of 1 lemon
1½	tablespoons cornstarch
	Chopped chives or parsley

1. *Cook veal:* Place veal in a large Dutch oven. Stick clove into onion, then add to pan with carrots. Using kitchen string, tie celery, parsley, and thyme in a bundle to make a bouquet garni; add to pan. Season lightly with salt and pepper, then add water to cover. Bring to a boil over medium-high heat; cover, reduce heat, and simmer until very tender when pierced, 1 hour for veal breast to 1¾ hours for shanks.

2. *Sauté onions and mushrooms:* In a wide skillet, melt butter in oil over medium heat. Add onions and mushrooms; cook, stirring often, until mushrooms are lightly browned and onions are tender when pierced. Remove from heat and season lightly with salt and pepper.

3. *Make sauce:* Remove veal from cooking liquid, reserving liquid in pan. When veal is cool enough to handle, remove meat from bones, discarding bones. Cut veal into 1- by 2-inch pieces, place in a pan, cover lightly, and keep warm in a 250°F oven. Remove and discard bouquet garni, carrots, and onion from liquid. Bring liquid to a boil over medium-high heat, then boil, stirring often, until liquid is reduced by half. In a small bowl, mix crème fraîche, lemon juice, and cornstarch until smooth. Whisk crème fraîche mixture into cooking liquid and bring to a boil. Strain into another pan and mix in onions and mushrooms. Reheat, if necessary, and season to taste with salt and pepper.

4. *Serve:* Divide veal into warm, wide, shallow bowls; spoon sauce evenly over veal. Sprinkle with chives.

Note: Blanquette may be accompanied by steamed rice or potatoes.

Eric Ripert

SAUTÉED GROUPER ON MUSHROOM PURÉE

With Sherry Vinegar, Bacon, and Black Pepper Sauce, and Roasted Portobello with Garlic and Herbs
4 Servings

Sherry Vinegar Sauce

4	cups chicken stock
2	thick slices double-smoked bacon, cut into ⅛- by 1-inch strips
¼	cup finely diced shallot
½	cup aged sherry wine vinegar
¼	cup (2 oz.) unsalted butter
1½	teaspoons coarsely cracked pepper
	Fine sea salt

Mushrooms

3	large portobello mushrooms (each about 3½-in. diameter)
½	cup extra-virgin olive oil
5	cloves garlic, coarsely chopped
2	sprigs rosemary
	Fine sea salt and freshly ground white pepper
2	tablespoons butter
¼	cup chicken stock

Sautéed Grouper

2	tablespoons corn oil
4	grouper fillets (about 7 oz. each), rinsed and patted dry
	Fine sea salt and freshly ground white pepper

1. *Make sauce:* In a 2½- to 3-quart pan, bring chicken stock to a boil over medium-high heat; boil, watching carefully, until reduced to 1 cup liquid. Meanwhile, in 1½-quart pan, cook bacon over medium heat until crisp. Lift out bacon and drain on paper towels. Discard all but 1 tablespoon of the drippings in pan. To drippings add shallot and cook until softened, about 1 minute. Add vinegar and boil, stirring occasionally, until most of the liquid is gone. Add reduced chicken stock, increase heat to medium-high, and bring to a boil. Whisk in butter, then stir in bacon and pepper; season to taste with salt. Set sauce aside.

2. *Roast mushrooms:* Remove and discard mushroom stems; peel and discard thin skin from mushroom caps. Place mushrooms smooth side up in a shallow baking pan, drizzle with olive oil to coat well, then scatter garlic over mushrooms; cut rosemary sprigs in half, and distribute over the mushrooms. Season with salt and pepper. Roast in a 400°F oven until mushrooms release their liquid, about 15 minutes. Discard garlic and rosemary. Let cool briefly.

3. *Make mushroom purée:* In food processor or blender, combine 1 of the roasted mushrooms, butter, and chicken stock. Whirl until very smooth; set purée aside.

4. *Cook fish:* Heat 1 tablespoon of corn oil in each of two 10-inch skillets over high heat just until oil begins to smoke. Season grouper fillets with salt and pepper. Cook, 2 to a pan, until browned and crusty on first sides, about 3 minutes; turn carefully and cook until a skewer inserted into thickest part of fillet for 5 seconds feels hot when touched, about 4 minutes longer.

5. *Serve:* Reheat sauce briefly, if necessary. Cut each roasted mushroom into 4 pieces. For each serving, place 2 mushroom quarters on the upper right side of plate, then spread 1 tablespoon mushroom purée in a strip diagonally across the plate from top left to bottom right. Place a grouper fillet in the middle of the purée strip, a little to the left of the center. Spoon 2 tablespoons of sauce over the fish.

Guenter Seeger

GRILLED JOHN DORY FILLETS

With Glazed Turnips, Steeped Prunes, and Rosemary Snow
6 Servings

1	pound pitted prunes
1	whole clove
10	whole black peppercorns
2	vanilla beans
1	star anise pod
1	cardamom pod
3	orange slices
2	lemon slices
1	bottle (750 ml) Pinot Noir or other dry red wine
4	cups lowfat milk
8	fresh rosemary sprigs
1	pound baby turnips with tops, peeled and trimmed
1	teaspoon powdered sugar
¼	cup butter
6	pieces (6 to 7 oz. each) John Dory fillets, rinsed and patted dry
	Salt and freshly ground pepper
2	tablespoons finely chopped parsley

Special equipment: 1-quart or larger heatproof jar, hand-held (stick-type) blender

1. *Steep prunes:* Place prunes in a heat-proof jar, 1-quart size or larger. Add clove, peppercorns, vanilla beans, star anise, cardamom, orange slices, and lemon slices. Bring wine to a boil in a 2-quart pan, then pour over prunes. Cover and let prunes steep for at least 8 hours or up to 1 day.

2. *Steep milk and rosemary:* Pour milk into a 1½- to 2-quart pan; place over low heat until warm. Add rosemary and let steep over lowest heat for 30 minutes.

3. *Cook turnips:* In a 2- to 3-quart pan, combine turnips, powdered sugar, butter, and about ½ cup water. Bring to a boil over high heat, then reduce heat, cover, and boil gently until turnips are tender when pierced, about 10 minutes. Uncover and continue to cook until most of the liquid is gone and turnips take on a golden glaze. Remove from heat and keep warm while cooking fish.

4. *Grill fish and prunes:* Remove 12 to 18 prunes from wine mixture and pat dry. Season fish fillets with salt and pepper to taste. Place fish on a well-seasoned grill or large cast-iron skillet; cook, carefully turning once, until just opaque but still moist in thickest part (cut to test), 8 to 10 minutes total. Add prunes to grill around the fish after you turn fillets.

5. *Make rosemary snow:* Remove and discard rosemary from milk. Using a hand-held (stick-type) blender, beat warm milk until a thick foam forms on top.

6. *Serve:* Lightly mix turnips with parsley. On each plate, place a fish fillet in center, then garnish with turnips and prunes. Scoop foam from surface of milk and place a spoonful on each fish fillet.

Joachim Splichal

LOIN OF RABBIT WITH POTATO AND BACON HASH

4 Servings

2	medium-size potatoes (6 to 8 oz. each), peeled and cut into ⅓-inch cubes
1½ to 2 cups brown chicken stock (page 193)
3½	ounces bacon, cut into ⅓-inch cubes
6	boneless rabbit loins
	Olive oil for frying
3½	tablespoons butter
2	shallots, diced
	Kidney and liver of 1 rabbit, finely diced
	Salt and freshly ground pepper
½	cup chopped parsley
4	quail eggs
	Extra-virgin olive oil

1. *Cook potatoes:* Cook potatoes in boiling salted water just until tender, about 5 minutes; drain well and set aside.

2. *Reduce chicken stock:* In a small pan, bring chicken stock to a boil and reduce until concentrated to ¾ cup; set aside.

3. *Render bacon:* In a wide skillet over medium heat, cook bacon until fat has cooked out and bacon begins to brown. With a slotted spoon, lift out bacon cubes and drain on paper towels; discard drippings.

4. *Prepare rabbit loins:* Cut 2 of the rabbit loins into ⅓-inch cubes; set aside. To skillet add enough olive oil to cover pan bottom; increase heat to medium-high. Brown remaining whole rabbit loins well in oil on all sides. Remove from pan and keep warm.

5. *Make hash:* In same pan, melt 2 table-spoons of the butter and add potatoes and shallots. Cook, lifting and turning with a wide spatula, until potatoes are golden brown on all sides. Add bacon cubes and rabbit cubes and sauté for 1 minute longer. Stir in rabbit kidney and liver and concentrated chicken stock. Season to taste with salt and pepper. Bring to a boil and remove from heat. Lightly mix in parsley.

6. *Serve:* Divide potato and bacon mixture onto 4 warm plates. Slice seared rabbit loins and arrange around potatoes. Melt remaining 1½ tablespoons butter in a small nonstick skillet over medium heat. Add quail eggs, one at a time, and cook just until set, about 45 seconds. As each egg cooks, place it atop a serving of potatoes. Drizzle a few drops of extra-virgin olive oil over each serving.

Charlie Trotter

SEA SCALLOPS WITH FRESH SOYBEANS

4 Servings

Tofu

¾	cup diced firm tofu
1	tablespoon lemon juice
2	teaspoons thinly sliced cilantro leaves
1	teaspoon sesame seeds, toasted (see note)
1½	tablespoons tamari
4	teaspoons Asian sesame oil
1	tablespoon mirin (sweet rice wine)

Soybeans

1½	cups shelled fresh soybeans (edamame)
¼	cup olive oil
1	tablespoon unseasoned rice vinegar
	Salt and pepper

Garnishes

4	fresh water chestnuts
2	teaspoons dried hijiki seaweed
2	tablespoons micro cilantro sprouts or arugula

Scallops

8	large sea scallops, rinsed and patted dry
	Fleur de sel
	Freshly ground pepper
1	tablespoon grapeseed oil

1. *Prepare tofu:* In a small bowl, combine tofu, lemon juice, and sliced cilantro. Let stand at room temperature for 15 minutes.

2. *Prepare soybeans:* Add soybeans to boiling salted water in a small pan and blanch until tender when pierced, about 2 minutes. Drain and place in a bowl of ice water until cool. Remove and discard outer membrane from each bean. In food processor, combine soybeans, olive oil, and the 1 tablespoon rice vinegar; whirl until smooth, adding water if necessary to make a thick purée. Season to taste with salt and pepper. Set aside until ready to serve.

3. *Prepare garnishes:* Add water chestnuts to boiling water in a small pan and cook for 1 to 2 minutes; drain and peel. Slice thin, then cut into thin strips. Place hijiki in a small bowl, cover with water, and let stand until soft; drain well.

4. *Prepare plates:* Heat soybean purée in a small nonstick pan. Transfer tofu mixture to another small nonstick pan. Add sesame seeds, tamari, sesame oil, and mirin. Heat tofu mixture until warmed through. For each serving, spoon a dollop of the hot soybeans into center of each plate; keep warm.

5. *Cook scallops:* Season scallops to taste with fleur de sel and pepper. Heat grapeseed oil in a wide skillet over high heat. Add scallops and cook, turning once, just until well browned but still moist in center (cut to test), about 3 minutes total.

6. *Serve:* For each serving, arrange 2 scallops over soybean purée. Scatter the tofu and water chestnuts around the purée; drizzle with tofu juices. Sprinkle with cilantro sprouts and drained hijiki.

Note: To toast sesame seeds, place in a small pan over medium heat until fragrant and golden, 4 to 5 minutes.

Norman Van Aken

MIXED SEAFOOD PIE WITH CORN CRUST

One 12-inch pie, 6 to 8 servings

Seafood Filling

1	poblano chile
3	tablespoons butter
2	cups (½-inch pieces) seeded, peeled calabaza or acorn squash
1	teaspoon cumin seeds, toasted and ground (see note)
1	tablespoon sugar
	Kosher salt and freshly toasted and ground pepper (see note)
2	cups fresh corn kernels
⅓	cup oil-cured black olives, pitted and coarsely chopped
½	cup crumbled or diced cooked chorizo or other spicy sausage
12	ounces snapper fillets, rinsed and patted dry
12	ounces sea bass fillets, rinsed and patted dry
12	ounces sea scallops, rinsed and patted dry
2	tablespoons olive oil
4	cloves garlic, sliced
4	shallots, minced
¼	cup chopped flat-leaf parsley
1½	cups dry white wine, such as Sauvignon Blanc
1	cup sour cream
½	cup soft bread crumbs

Corn Crust

3½	tablespoons butter
2	cloves garlic, sliced
2½	cups fresh corn kernels
1	large egg yolk
1	large egg
¼	cup milk
¼	cup all-purpose flour
½	teaspoon baking powder
1	teaspoon salt
6	green onions, minced
1	jalapeño chile, stemmed, seeded, and minced
	Kosher salt and freshly toasted and ground black pepper (see note)

1. *Prepare poblano chile:* Rotate chile over flame on gas range until charred and blistered, 1 to 1½ minutes; or place on a baking sheet 3 inches below broiler and broil, turning often, until blistered, 6 to 8 minutes. Place roasted chile in a plastic bag, seal tightly, and let stand until cool enough to handle. Peel off the skin, then remove and discard stem and seeds. Finely chop chile and set aside.

2. *Bake squash and corn for filling:* Melt 1 tablespoon of the butter. In a medium bowl, mix squash, the melted butter, ground cumin, and sugar. Season to taste with salt and pepper. Transfer mixture to a shallow baking pan. Bake in a 375°F oven until squash is tender when pierced, 25 to 35 minutes. Add corn, mix lightly, and return to oven. Bake for 10 minutes longer. Remove pan from oven and add chopped poblano, olives, and chorizo; set aside. Reduce oven temperature to 350°F.

3. *Cook fish and scallops:* Cut snapper and sea bass into 1-inch pieces. Season fish and scallops with salt and pepper to taste. In an oven-proof 12-inch nonstick sauté pan over medium-high heat, melt 1 tablespoon of the butter in the olive oil. When butter foams, add scallops and brown well, turning once after 1 to 1½ minutes; cook until golden on undersides, about 1 minute longer. Carefully lift scallops onto a plate; set aside. To same pan, add fish and sauté, shaking pan gently to prevent sticking, until browned. Remove fish from pan with a slotted spatula (leave drippings in pan) and transfer to a plate; set aside.

4. *Make sauce:* Add remaining 1 tablespoon butter to pan in which seafood was cooked. Reduce heat to moderate and add garlic and shallots; cook, stirring, for 1 minute. Stir in parsley and wine. Increase heat to medium-high and boil, stirring often, until liquid is reduced to ½ cup. Stir in any juices that have accumulated with the seafood, and cook for 1 to 2 minutes longer. Remove pan from heat and whisk in sour cream. Season to taste with salt and pepper.

5. *Complete filling:* Cut scallops into bite-size pieces. To sauce, add scallops, fish, and squash mixture.

6. *Make corn crust:* Wash and dry sauté pan in which sauce and seafood were cooked. In it, melt 2 tablespoons of the butter over medium-high heat. Add garlic and cook for 1 minute; then add corn and cook for 3 to 4 minutes longer. Remove from heat and let stand until cooled. Transfer corn mixture to a blender or food processor; set pan aside to use for baking the pie (step 8). To corn, add egg yolk, egg, and milk; whirl until smooth. In a medium bowl, sift together flour, baking powder, and the 1 teaspoon salt. Fold in the corn mixture until batter is smooth. Set batter aside.

7. *Make topping:* In a small skillet over medium heat, melt remaining 1½ tablespoons butter. Add green onions and jalapeño; cook, stirring until jalapeño is bright green and begins to soften, about 2 minutes. Remove from heat and season to taste with salt and pepper.

8. *Bake seafood pie:* Wipe out the pan in which corn was cooked. Sprinkle bread crumbs over bottom of pan. Spread the seafood filling over the crumbs. Lightly but evenly spread the corn batter over the seafood filling. Sprinkle the sautéed green onion mixture over corn batter. Bake in 350°F oven until center of the pie springs back when lightly touched, about 50 minutes.

9. *Serve:* Spoon hot pie onto warm plates.

Note: To toast peppercorns, place in a small pan over medium heat until fragrant, 4 to 5 minutes.